The Metropolitan Opera Presents

Georges Bizet's

Carmen

Emma Calvé as Carmen, 1893
Falk / Metropolitan Opera Archives

The Metropolitan Opera Presents

Georges Bizet's

Carmen

Music by Georges Bizet

Libretto by Henri Meilhac and Ludovic Halévy

Based on the novella by Prosper Mérimée

**AMADEUS
PRESS**
An Imprint of Hal Leonard Corporation

The **Met**
ropolitan
Opera

Published in 2014 by Amadeus Press
An Imprint of Hal Leonard Corporation
7777 West Bluemound Road
Milwaukee, WI 53213

Trade Book Division Editorial Offices
33 Plymouth St., Montclair, NJ 07042

English translation of libretto copyright © 1999 by Leyerle Publications, 28 Stanley Street, Mt. Morris, New York 14510. English translation by Nico Castel. Originally published by Leyerle Publications as part of *French Opera Libretti*. These publications, and others in the Leyerle Opera Libretti series, are available directly from Leyerle's website at www.leyerlepublications.com.

Printed in the United States of America

Book design by Mark Lerner

Library of Congress Cataloging-in-Publication Data is available upon request.

ISBN 978-1-57467-462-0

www.amadeuspress.com

CONTENTS

Italo Campanini as Don José, 1884
Mora / Metropolitan Opera Archives

INTRODUCTION

Strong-willed, fiery, and tempestuous—the character of Carmen has captivated the world's imagination for more than a century and a half. The beautiful gypsy first came to life in Prosper Mérimée's 1845 novella and became immortal through Bizet's opera 30 years later. The composer, though, didn't live to see his opera triumph around the world. He died just three months after its Paris premiere, which was not a success, due mostly to the unexpectedly realistic and sensual story that came as a shock to 19th-century audiences. The Met first presented *Carmen* in its inaugural 1883–84 season, when it was already an international hit, and has since performed it nearly a thousand times.

Like the previous volumes of the Metropolitan Opera Presents series, this book is designed to give you an in-depth introduction to Bizet's immortal creation. In addition to the complete libretto in French and English, you will find a synopsis, a detailed program note with historical background, and the "In Focus" feature we provide in the Met's house program every night—a brief summary of key aspects of the opera. We've also included many archival photos of some of the greatest stars who have appeared at the Met in 130 years of *Carmen* history. Whether you watch the opera in the theater or as part of our *Live in HD* movie-theater transmissions, or listen to a radio broadcast or web stream, we hope this book will give you all the information you need to enjoy and appreciate Carmen's many riches.

To learn more about Met productions, Live in HD *movie-theater transmissions,* Met membership, and more, visit metopera.org.

The Metropolitan Opera Presents

Georges Bizet's

Carmen

THE RAY

VOL. 13.   BOSTON, SATURDAY, JANUARY 5, 1884   No. 112

BOSTON THEATRE

TOMPKINS & HILL .... Proprietors
EUGENE TOMPKINS .... Manager

MR. HENRY E. ABBEY'S

Grand Italian Opera Company

FROM THE

METROPOLITAN OPERA HOUSE, NEW YORK.

ACTING MANAGER . . . . . . MR. MAURICE GRAU

THIS EVENING

BIZET'S OPERA,

CARMEN !

DON JOSE	Sig. CAMPANINI
ESCAMILLO (Toreador)	Sig. DEL PUENTE
IL DANCAIRO	Sig. CORSINI
IL REMENDADO	Sig. GRAZZI
ZUNIGA	Sig. AUGIER
MORALES	Sig. CONTINI
MICHAELA	Mme. VALLERIA
PAQUITA	Mlle. CORANI
MERCEDES	Mlle. L. LABLACHE

—AND—

CARMEN, a Gypsy	Mme. TREBELLI

The Incidental Divertisement will be supported by Mme. MALVINA CAVALAZZI and Corps de Ballet.

Conductor	Sig. CLEOFONTE CAMPANINI

The Costumes are entirely new, and were manufactured at Venice by D. ASCOLI, under the supervision of Mr. HENRY DAZIAN.

Stage Managers	MM. CORANI and ABBIATI
Treasurer	Mr. CHARLES H. MATHEWS
Business Manager	Mr. MARCUS R. MAYER

MONDAY EVENING, Jan. 7 --- The Eminent Favorite,

JOHN McCULLOUGH

As VIRGINIUS, the Roman Father.

The Pianos used at this Theatre are from the celebrated manufactory of CHICKERING & SONS. The Cabinet Organs are from the manufacturers, MASON & HAMLIN.

The WEBER Pianos are used by Mr. Abbey's Opera Company.

OPERA GLASSES TO LET AT THE STAND IN THE FRONT LOBBY

DOORS OPEN AT 1.30 and 7.15. . . . . BEGINS AT 2 and 7.45

ogram for the   ur at the
oston Theatre
ETROPOLITAN O

Synopsis

Act I

Spain, around 1830. In Seville by a cigarette factory, soldiers comment on the townspeople. Among them is Micaëla, a peasant girl, who asks for a corporal named Don José. Moralès, another corporal, tells her he will return with the changing of the guard. The relief guard, headed by Lieutenant Zuniga, soon arrives, and José learns from Moralès that Micaëla has been looking for him. When the factory bell rings, the men of Seville gather to watch the female workers—especially their favorite, the gypsy Carmen. She tells her admirers that love is free and obeys no rules. Only one man pays no attention to her: Don José. Carmen throws a flower at him, and the girls go back to work. José picks up the flower and hides it when Micaëla returns. She brings a letter from José's mother, who lives in a village in the countryside. As he begins to read the letter, Micaëla leaves. José is about to throw away the flower when a fight erupts inside the factory between Carmen and another girl. Zuniga sends José to retrieve the gypsy. Carmen refuses to answer Zuniga's questions, and José is ordered to take her to prison. Left alone with him, she entices José with suggestions of a rendezvous at Lillas Pastia's tavern. Mesmerized, he agrees to let her get away. As they leave for prison, Carmen escapes. Don José is arrested.

Act II

Carmen and her friends Frasquita and Mercédès entertain the guests at the tavern. Zuniga tells Carmen that José has just been released. The bullfighter Escamillo enters, boasting about the pleasures of his profession, and flirts with Carmen, who tells him that she is involved with someone else. After the tavern guests have left with Escamillo, the smugglers Dancaïre and Remendado explain their latest scheme to the women. Frasquita and Mercédès are willing to help, but Carmen refuses because she is in love. The smugglers withdraw as José approaches. Carmen arouses his jealousy by telling him how she danced for Zuniga. She dances for him now, but when a bugle call is heard he says he must return to the barracks. Carmen mocks him. To prove his love, José shows her the flower she threw at him and confesses how its scent made him not lose hope during the weeks in prison. She is unimpressed: if he really loved her, he would desert the army and join her in a life of freedom in the mountains. José refuses, and Carmen tells him to leave. Zuniga bursts in, and in a jealous rage José fights him. The smugglers return and disarm Zuniga. José now has no choice but to join them.

Act III

Carmen and José quarrel in the smugglers' mountain hideaway. She admits that her love is fading and advises him to return to live with his mother. When Frasquita and Mercédès turn the cards to tell their fortunes, they foresee love and riches for themselves, but Carmen's cards spell death—for her and for José. Micaëla appears, frightened by the mountains and afraid to meet the woman who has turned José into a criminal. She hides when a shot rings out. José has fired at an intruder, who turns out to be Escamillo. He tells José that he has come to find Carmen, and the two men fight. The smugglers separate them, and Escamillo invites everyone, Carmen in particular, to his next bullfight. When he has left, Micaëla emerges and begs José to return home. He agrees when he learns that his mother is dying, but before he leaves he warns Carmen that they will meet again.

Act IV

Back in Seville, the crowd cheers the bullfighters on their way to the arena. Carmen arrives on Escamillo's arm, and Frasquita and Mercédès warn her that José is nearby. Unafraid, she waits outside the entrance as the crowds enter the arena. José appears and begs Carmen to forget the past and start a new life with him. She calmly tells him that their affair is over: she was born free and free she will die. The crowd is heard cheering Escamillo. José keeps trying to win Carmen back. She takes off his ring and throws it at his feet before heading for the arena. José stabs her to death.

Geraldine Farrar as Carmen and Enrico Caruso as Don José, 1914

In Focus

William Berger

Premiere: Opéra Comique, Paris; March 3, 1875

Bizet's masterpiece of the gypsy seductress who lives by her own rules, no matter what the cost, has had an impact far beyond the opera house. The opera's melodic sweep is as irresistible as the title character herself, a force of nature who has become a defining female cultural figure. This drama of a soldier torn between doing the right thing and the woman he cannot resist bursts with melody and seethes with all the erotic vitality of its unforgettable title character. *Carmen* was a scandal at its premiere and was roundly denounced in the press for its flagrant immorality. The power of the music and the drama, however, created an equally vocal faction in favor of the work. The composer Tchaikovsky and the philosopher Nietzsche both praised the opera, the latter identifying in the robustness of the score nothing less than a cure-all for the world's spiritual ills.

The Creators

Georges Bizet (1838–1875) was a French composer whose talent was apparent from childhood. *Carmen* was his final work, and its success was still uncertain at the time of his premature death (although the opera was not quite the total failure in its initial run that it has sometimes been called). Henri Meilhac (1831–1897) was a librettist and dramatist who would subsequently provide the libretto for Jules Massenet's popular *Manon* (1884). His collaborator on *Carmen* was Ludovic Halévy (1834–1908), the nephew of Jacques Fromental Halévy (composer of the opera *La Juive* and Bizet's father-in-law). Composer Ernest Guiraud (1837–1892), born in New Orleans, was a friend of Bizet's who wrote the recitatives between the set numbers when *Carmen* moved from the Opéra Comique (where dialogue was customary) to the opera houses of the world. The libretto of *Carmen* is based on a novella by Prosper Mérimée (1803–1870), a French dramatist, historian, and archaeologist. According to one of his letters, the book was inspired by a true story that the Countess of Montijo told him during a visit to Spain. Published in 1845, it was Mérimée's most popular work.

The Setting

The opera takes place in and around Seville, a city that, by the time *Carmen* was written, had already served many operatic composers as an exotic setting conducive to erotic intrigues and turmoil (Rossini's *Il Barbiere di Siviglia* and Verdi's *La Forza del Destino,* among others). The hometown of Don Juan, the city also inspired Mozart with *Don Giovanni,* and Beethoven used Seville as the setting for a study of marital fidelity in *Fidelio. Carmen* is particularly associated with this beguiling city of colorful processions, bullfights, and a vibrant gypsy community.

The Music

The score of *Carmen* contains so many instantly recognizable melodies that it can be easy to overlook how well constructed it is. The orchestra brings to life a broad palette of sound. The major solos are excellent combinations of arresting melody and dramatic purpose, most notably the baritone's famous Toréador Song, the tenor's wrenching Flower Song in Act II, and Micaëla's soaring Act

III aria. Carmen and the lead tenor have three remarkable duets marking the stages of their fateful relationship: the seductive phase (Act I), conflict (Act II), and tragic explosion (Act IV). Unlike in traditional operatic duets, however, they almost never sing at the same time, a device that emphasizes their inherently disparate natures. Interestingly, while Carmen has several solos in the form of songs—that is, moments in which the character is actually supposed to be singing within the context of the drama—she has no actual aria. It's a dramaturgical device that suggests she is seen first as a sort of celebrity, performing for others, and then as a projection of the fantasies of others.

Carmen at the Met

Carmen entered the standard Met repertoire slowly, premiering on tour in Boston in 1884, sung in Italian. After several performances in German, it finally became a Met staple in the original French in 1893 with Emma Calvé, her generation's leading interpreter of the title role, who performed the part more than 130 times with the Met before 1904. Enrico Caruso sang the lead tenor role between 1906 and 1919, and the charismatic Geraldine Farrar appeared as the gypsy temptress from 1914 to 1922 (she also played the role in a popular silent movie of 1915). In more recent decades, famous Met Carmens have included Risë Stevens (1945–1961), Marilyn Horne (1972–1988), Denyce Graves (1995–2005), and Olga Borodina (2000–2010). Among the memorable tenors to perform in the opera were Giovanni Martinelli (1915–1941), Richard Tucker (1952–1972), James McCracken (1966–1975), Plácido Domingo (1971–1997), and Neil Shicoff (2000–2004). Leonard Bernstein conducted *Carmen* for the opening night of the 1972–1973 season, and Music Director James Levine has led more than 40 performances dating back to 1986. The current production by Richard Eyre opened on New Year's Eve 2009, with Elīna Garanča, Roberto Alagna, Barbara Frittoli, and Mariusz Kwiecien in the leading roles, with Yannick Nézet-Séguin conducting.

Angelo Badà as Remendado, Lenora Sparkes as Frasquita,
Geraldine Farrar as Carmen, Sophie Braslau as Mercédès,
and Albert Reiss as Dancaïre, 1914–15
WHITE STUDIO

Program Note

Hugh Macdonald

The death of Georges Bizet on June 3, 1875, exactly three months after the famous opening night of *Carmen* at the Opéra Comique in Paris, is one of the cruelest ironies in the history of music. While it was certainly tragic that Puccini never lived to see *Turandot* and that Berlioz never lived to see *Les Troyens,* those composers were at the end of illustrious careers. Bizet was only 36 and had just revealed for the first time the true depth of his operatic genius. If Verdi, Wagner, or Strauss had died at that age, not many of their works would be heard in our opera houses today. Just a few extra months granted to Bizet would have shown him that the Vienna Opera had presented *Carmen* to a reception quite different from the shocked incomprehension that greeted it in Paris; just three more years would have given him the satisfaction of knowing that it had played in Brussels, Budapest, St. Petersburg, Stockholm, London, Dublin, New York, and Philadelphia, and he would at last have made a respectable living as a composer instead of having to toil over four-hand arrangements of lesser operas by lesser composers.

If only those pig-headed Parisians on the first night had been less parochial in their judgment, we like to think, success and recognition might have staved off the quinsy and rheumatism that led to

Bizet's death, probably precipitated by depression. Bizet was used to failure, since none of his theatrical ventures had been successful before. But none of them displayed the genius that lifts every page of *Carmen* to starry heights. His early works *Les Pêcheurs de Perles, La Jolie Fille de Perth,* and *Djamileh* all show glimpses of what he could do. In *Carmen* Bizet invested more energy and passion than ever before.

The crucial idea, Bizet's own, was to base the story on Prosper Mérimée's novella *Carmen.* In 1872, he was commissioned to write a three-act opera for the Opéra Comique, a theater where operas traditionally ended happily, with villainy and sin put firmly in their place; loyalty and fidelity were always rewarded. It was a family theater where audiences would be amused and entertained, excited even, but never shocked. The choice of *Carmen* inevitably led to an impasse, since the heroine is the villain and meets her death on stage. She flaunts her attractions and boasts of her conquests. She smokes, seduces soldiers, corrupts customs officials, and smuggles on the side. But she is fascinating, clever, beautiful, and sometimes even tender, and her music is so alluring that no one can escape her magnetism. French society lived out a convenient hypocrisy by indulging its fancies in private while maintaining a correct exterior. What people saw at the Opéra Comique was unfortunately very public: sensuality was presented here in the raw, to music of unmistakable appeal. Social mores have so radically changed in our century that the complexity of the response to *Carmen*—a mixture of distaste, fascination, and guilt—is not easy to disentangle.

Bizet was not attempting to engineer social change or storm the barricades of propriety; he simply recognized a good subject for music and knew he could bring it to life on the stage. This is musical theater charged with an unprecedented realism that makes the two principal figures, Carmen and Don José, as vivid as flesh and blood, destroyed by their appetites and their weaknesses. The librettists, Henri Meilhac and Ludovic Halévy (an experienced and expert team), made the story convincingly operatic by introducing two balancing characters, neither of any importance in Mérimée's story. First is Micaëla, whose purity, devotion to Don José, and attachment to his dying mother make Carmen's personality all the more striking and brazen. And Escamillo is the irresistible lure that entices Carmen from Don José, though the bullfighter, unlike the soldier, would never shed a tear over her infidelity.

The settings, too, are superbly theatrical: a square in Seville where soldiers change guard and cigarette girls gather; Lillas Pastia's tavern, where all forms of lowlife meet; the smugglers' hideout in the mountains; and finally the bullring where the slaughter of bulls inside (offstage) acts as dramatic counterpoint to José's desperate murder of Carmen outside (onstage). Carmen, as even she herself knows, is doomed. So too is José, by his defiance of military orders, by joining forces with the smugglers, and by his willful neglect of Micaëla and his mother, not to mention his fatal passion for Carmen. In Mérimée's version, he has also committed two murders.

Fearing that such a story would frighten off his loyal though dwindling public, Camille du Locle, director of the Opéra Comique, did his best to soften the blow by cautioning his public and steering high officials away. He could make nothing of the music, in any case, and described it as "Cochin-Chinese." Such counter-advertising by a theater manager is hard to believe. The librettists similarly seem to have been willing to tone down the impact of the work that would make their names immortal. Throughout the long rehearsal period from October 1874 to March 1875, Bizet had to resist pressure for change and suffer the complaints of both orchestra and chorus that it was not performable.

But the composer had supporters, since his two principal singers believed in the opera from the start. Paul Lhérie, the Don José, was full of good intentions, though he sang disastrously flat in his unaccompanied entrance in Act II. In Célestine Galli-Marié, Bizet had a superlative, perhaps definitive, Carmen. She evidently brought to the role the blend of sultry sensuality and fatal bravado that all good Carmens need; her own private life was liberated (by the standards of the day), and she is said to have had an affair with Bizet, which is not unlikely given the pressures under which they were working and the uncertain state of his marriage. Further support for Bizet came from one or two good notices in the press and a few expressions of admiration from fellow composers.

The majority of the notices after that first night, though, were hostile and uncomprehending, and one or two were deeply insulting. The show did not close, however. It ran for more than 40 performances, not at all a disgraceful total, kept alive no doubt by its salacious reputation and, after a dozen performances, by the sensational irony of Bizet's death. By the time the Opéra Comique dared to stage it again, in 1883, the opera was a worldwide success.

Part of *Carmen*'s appeal rests on its brilliant evocation of Spain. Bizet went to some trouble to find authentic melodies. The famous Habanera, for example, was adapted from a tune by the Spanish-American composer Sebastián Yradier. But Bizet could invent good Spanish music of his own, too. The Séguedille that closes Act I is superlatively colorful and dramatic, as is the gypsy song that opens the following act in Lillas Pastia's tavern.

Yet much of the opera is not Spanish at all. Whatever its novelty, it belongs to the tradition of French opéra comique, as we can tell when leading characters present themselves in two-verse songs, or couplets. The depiction of the two smugglers Dancaïre and Remendado as comic figures belongs to the same tradition. There is also a strong strain of French lyricism in *Carmen*, derived from Gounod, Bizet's mentor, who jokingly said that Micaëla's Act III aria was stolen from him. It faithfully echoes his style in such works as *Roméo et Juliette* (on which Bizet had worked as pianist and assistant).

Those critics in 1875 who could see beyond the sensation of the story to the music were confused. Conventions were stretched, and the dramatic immediacy of the music was stronger than anything they had heard before. Such departures from custom were invariably labeled "Wagnerian," a term of abuse in France at that time. Chromatic harmony and daring key shifts were assumed to be Wagner's monopoly. But Bizet had no intention whatsoever of imitating Wagner, whose music and theories he knew little about. His music was modern, and for many critics that was enough. His genius is evident in the brilliance of each individual number, finding sharply distinctive melodies and moods for every scene. Few other composers of the time could boast such fertile invention.

The French learned to love *Carmen,* but not before it had conquered the world's opera houses. In New York, it was first performed in Italian at the Academy of Music in 1878, then in English in 1881, reaching the Metropolitan Opera during its first season on January 5, 1884 (also still in Italian). It has remained in the Met's repertoire ever since, and may well be, as Tchaikovsky predicted, the most popular opera in the world.

Giovanni Martinelli as Don José, 1917
HERMAN MISHKIN / METROPOLITAN OPERA ARCHIVES

CARMEN[1]

PERSONNAGES

Moralès, brigadier: baryton
Micaëla, paysanne: soprano
Zuniga, lieutenant: basse
Don José, brigadier: ténor
Carmen, bohémienne: mezzo-soprano
Mercédès, bohémienne: mezzo-soprano
Frasquita, bohémienne: soprano
Le Remendado, contrebandier: ténor
Le Dancaïre, contrebandier: baryton
Escamillo, toréador: baryton

Filles de cigarettes, Cavalerie, un Aubergiste, Contrebandiers, Danseurs, Toréros, Picadors, les assistants de Matador, Policiers, Mesdames et Messieurs de Séville, Mendiants, Vendeurs de rue

CHARACTERS

Moralès, an officer: baritone
Micaëla, a peasant girl: soprano
Zuniga, a lieutenant of dragoons: bass
Don José, a corporal of dragoons: tenor

Carmen, a gypsy girl: mezzo-soprano
Mercédes, gypsy companion of Carmen: mezzo-soprano
Frasquita, gypsy companion of Carmen: soprano
Remendado, a smuggler: tenor
Dancairo, a smuggler: baritone
Escamillo, a bullfighter: baritone

Cigarette Girls, Dragoons, an Inkeeper, Smugglers, Dancers, Bullfighters, Picadors, Matador's Assistants, Policemen, Ladies and
Gentlemen of Seville, Beggars, Street Vendors

L'action se déroule à Séville, en Espagne, aux environs de 1820.
The action takes place in Seville, Spain, sometime around about 1820.

PREMIER ACTE
ACT 1

Grande place à Séville
A public square in Seville

(D'un côté se trouve l'entrée d'une usine de cigarettes, de l'autre côté, un poste de garde de soldats qui flânent sur. Personnes vont et viennent.)
(To one side is the entrance of a cigarette factory, to the other side, a guard-house with soldiers loitering about. People are coming and going.)

NO. 1 CHŒUR DES LES SOLDATS
NO. 1 CHORUS OF DRAGOONS

Sur la place chacun passe, chacun vient, chacun va;
On the square everyone passes by, everyone comes, everyone goes;

drôles de gens que ces gens-là.
droll people those people there.

MORALÈS
À la porte du corps de garde
At the door of the corps of the guard

pour tuer le temps,
to kill the time,

on fume, on jase, l'on regarde
we smoke, we chat, we watch

passer les passants.
going by the passers-by.
(we watch the passers-by.)

(Après quelques instants, Micaëla entre. Elle porte une jupe bleue et a tresses qui atteignent ses épaules. Elle hésite, un peu gêné, et cherche parmi les soldats avec les yeux.)
(After a few moments, Micaëla enters. She wears a blue skirt and has braids that reach her shoulders. She is hesitant, somewhat embarrassed, and searches among the soldiers with her eyes.)

LES SOLDATS et MORALÈS
DRAGOONS and MORALÈS
Sur la place, etc.
On the square, etc.

MORALÈS
(aux soldats)
(to the soldiers)
Regardez donc cette petite qui semble vouloir nous parler.
Look at then that pretty girl who seems to want to talk to us.

Voyez, elle tourne, elle hésite.
Look, she is turning, she hesitates.

LES SOLDATS
THE DRAGOONS
À son secours il faut aller.
To her help we must go.

MORALÈS
(à Micaëla)
(To Micaëla)
Que cherchez-vous, la belle?
What are you looking for, my pretty?

MICAËLA
Moi, je cherche un brigadier.
Me, I am looking for a brigadier.

MORALÈS
Je suis là! Voilà!
I am here! Voilà!

MICAËLA
Mon brigadier à moi s'appelle Don José . . . le connaissez-vous?
My brigadier (mine) is called Don José, him do you know?

MORALÈS
Don José, nous le connaissons tous.
Don José, we him know all of us.
(All of us know him.)

MICAËLA
Vraiment, est-il avec vous, je vous prie?
Really, is he with you, I you beg?

MORALÈS
Il n'est pas brigadier dans notre compagnie.
He is not brigadier in our company.

MICAËLA
(désolée)
(disappointed)
Alors, il n'est pas là.
Then he is not here.

MORALÈS
Non, ma charmante, il n'est pas là,
No, my charming one, he is not here,

mais tout à l'heure il y sera.
but very soon he here will be.

Il y sera quand la garde montante
He here will be when the guard arriving

remplacera la garde descendante.
will replace the guard leaving.
(He will be here when the troop of new guards replaces the old one.)

CHŒUR
CHORUS
Il y sera quand la garde montante remplacera la garde descendante.

MORALÈS
Mais en attendant qu'il vienne,
But while you wait till he comes,

voulez-vous, la belle enfant,
do you want, my lovely child,

voulez-vous prendre la peine
do you want to take the trouble

d'entrer chez nous un instant.[2]
of coming in with us for a moment.

MICAËLA
Chez vous!
With you!

MORALÈS
Chez nous.
With us.

MICAËLA
Non pas, grand merci, messieurs les soldats.
Not that, many thanks, gentlemen (the) soldiers.

MORALÈS
Entrez sans crainte, mignonne,
Come in without fear, (my) pretty one,

je vous promets qu'on aura
I promise you that we will have

pour votre chère personne
for your dear person

tous les égards qu'il faudra.
all the consideration that is needed.

MICAËLA
Je n'en doute pas; cependant
I have no doubt about it; however

je reviendrai, c'est plus prudent.
I will return, it's more prudent

(reprenant en riant la phrase du sergeant)
(gently mocking the prhase of Moralès before)

Je reviendrai.
I will come back.

quand la garde montante remplacera la garde descendante.

LES SOLDATS
SOLDIERS
(entourant Micaëla)
(surrounding Micaëla)
Vous resterez.
You will stay.

MICAËLA
Non pas!
Not at all!

Au revoir, messieurs les soldats.
Farewell, misters (the) soldiers.
(Farewell, soldiers.)

(Elle s'échappe et se sauve en courant.)
(She hurries off.)

MORALÈS
L'oiseau s'envole, on s'en console,
The bird has escaped, we must be resigned,

reprenons notre passe-temps,
let us take up again our pastime,

et regardons passer les gens.
and let us watch pass the people.

LES SOLDATS
SOLDIERS
Sur la place chacun passe, etc.
On the square everyone passes, etc.

NO. 2 CHŒUR DES GAMINS
NO. 2 CHORUS OF URCHINS

(On entend au loin une marche militaire, clairons et fifres. C'est la garde montante qui arrive; un officier sort du poste. Les soldats du poste vont prendre leurs fusils et se rangent en ligne devant le corps de garde. Les passants forment un groupe pour assister à la parade. La marche militaire se rapproche. La garde montante débouche enfin et traverse le pont. Deux clairons et deux fifres d'abord. Puis une bande de petits gamins. Derrière les enfants, le Lieutenant Zuniga et le Brigadier Don José, puis les dragons.)
(The crowd, which has been watching the scene with Micaëla, now resumes its strolling. One hears from offstage a military march. It is the relief guard arriving. An officer comes out of the guardhouse and the other soldiers take their lances and form in ranks. The relief guard appears from one side and is preceded by a group of street urchins who imitate the marching of the soldiers.)

CHŒUR DES GAMINS
CHORUS OF URCHINS
Avec la garde montante,
With the guard mounting,

nous arrivons, nous voilà.
we arrive, we, there!

Sonne trompette éclatante, taratata;
Sound (the) trumpet ringing, taratata;

nous marchons la tête haute comme de petits soldats,
we march the head high like some little soldiers,

marquant sans faire de faute
marking without making mistakes

une, deux, marquant le pas.
one, two, marking the step.

Les épaules en arrière, et la poitrine en dehors,
The shoulders back and the chest out,

les bras de cette manière
the arms in this fashion

tombant tout le long du corps;
falling all along the body;

avec la garde montante, etc.
with the guard mounting, etc.

(La garde montante va se ranger à droite en face de la garde descendante. Les officiers se salient de l'épée et se mettent à causer à voix basse. On relève les sentinelles.)
(The new guard takes over from the old. The officers greet one another and speak in low voices.)

MORALÈS
(à Don José)
(to José)
Une jeune fille charmante
A young girl charming

vient de nous demander si tu n'étais pas là.
did of us ask if you were not here.

Jupe bleue et natte tombante.
Skirt blue and tresses falling.

JOSÉ
Ce doit être Micaëla.
It must be Micaëla.

(La garde descendante passe devant la garde montante. Les gamins en troupe reprennent la place qu'ils occupaient derrière les tambours et les fifres de la garde montante.)
(The trumpets blare and the troopes of guards exchange places. The urchins form in ranks and repeat their marching.)

GAMINS
URCHINS
Et la garde descendante
And the guard that's leaving

rentre chez elle et s'en va.
returns to its barracks and leaves.

Sonne, trompette éclatante, etc.

(Soldats, gamins et curieux s'éloignent par le fond; chœur, fifres et clairons vont diminuant. L'officier de la garde montante, pendant ce temps, passe silencieusement l'inspection de ses hommes. Quand le chœur des gamins a cessé de se faire entendre, les soldats rentrent dans le corps de garde. Don José et Zuniga restent seuls en scène.)
(Soldiers, urchins and the curious go off. An officer inspects the new guard. Soldiers stack their lances and go inside the barrack. José and Zuniga are left alone on stage.)

ZUNIGA
C'est bien là, n'est-ce pas, dans ce grand bâtiment
It is there, is it not, in that big building

que travaillent les cigarières?
that work the cigarette girls?
(girl cigarette makers?)

JOSÉ
C'est là, mon officier, et bien certainement
That's right, my officer, and most certainly

on ne vit nulle part filles aussi légères.
one has not seen any place girls so of easy virtue.

ZUNIGA
Mais au moins sont-elles jolies?
But at least are they pretty?

JOSÉ
Mon officier, je n'en sais rien,
Sir, I don't know,

et m'occupe assez peu de ces galanteries.
and I bother very little over those gallantries.

ZUNIGA
Ce qui t'occupe, ami, je le sais bien,
That which concerns you, friend, I know very well,

une jeune fille charmante, qu'on appelle Micaëla,
a young girl, charming, by name Micaëla,

jupe bleue et natte tombante.
skirt blue and tresses long.

Tu ne réponds rien à cela?
You don't answer anything to that?
(Have you anything to say to that?)

JOSÉ
Je réponds que c'est vrai, je réponds que je l'aime!
I answer that it's true, I answer that I love her!

Quant aux ouvrières d'ici,
as for factory girls here,

quant à leur beauté, les voici!
As for their beauty, there they are!

Et vous pouvez juger vous-même.
And you can judge them for yourself.

(La place se remplit de jeunes gens qui viennent se placer sur le passage des cigarières. Les soldats sortent du poste. Don José s'assied sur une chaise, et reste là fort indifférent à toutes ces allées et venues, travaillant à son épinglette.)
(The square fills with young men coming to watch the cigarette girls during their break. Soldiers come out from the guardhouse. Don José sits down and, indifferent to the scene, begins working on a small chain for his weapon.)

NO. 3 CHŒUR DES CIGARIÈRES JEUNES, GENS
NO. 3 CHORUS OF CIGARETTE GIRLS, YOUNG MEN

JEUNES GENS
YOUNG MEN
La cloche a sonné; nous, des ouvrières
The bell has rung, (and) we the factory girls

nous venons ici guetter le retour;
we come here watch their return;
(The bell has run and we've come here to gatch a glimpse of the factory girls as they return to the street;)

et nous vous suivons, brunes cigarières,
and we follow you, dark cigarette girls,

en vous murmurant des propos d'amour.
while to you murmuring some words of love.

(À ce moment paraissent les cigarières, la cigarette aux lèvres.)
(At this moment the cigarette workers appear, strolling languidly, cigarettes dangling from their mouths.)

LES SOLDATS
SOLDIERS
Voyez-les! Regards impudents, mines coquettes,
Look at them! Stares impudent, appearance coquettish,

fumant toutes du bout des dents la cigarette.
smoking all of them, from the end of their teeth the cigarette.
(Look at them! How impudently they stare, tempting coquettes, cigarettes dangling from their teeth.)

LES CIGARIÈRES
CIGARETTE GIRLS
Dans l'air, nous suivons des yeux la fumée,
In the air we follow with our eyes the smoke,

qui vers les cieux monte parfumée.
which toward the skies rises fragrant.

Cela monte gentiment à la tête,
It rises gently to your head,

tout doucement cela vous met l'âme en fête.
very softly it puts your soul in a gay mood.

Le doux parler des amants, c'est fumée!
The sweet talk of lovers is but smoke!

Leurs transports et leurs serments, c'est fumée![3]
Their rapture and their vows are smoke!

JEUNES GENS
YOUNG MEN
(Pour les filles de l'usine)
(To the factory girls)[4]
Sans faire les cruelles, écoutez-nous les belles,
Without playing the cruel ones, hear us out, my lovelies,

ô vous que nous adorons, que nous idolatrons!
oh you whom we adore, whom we idolize!

CHŒUR
CHORUS
Mais nous ne voyons pas la Carmencita!
But we still do not see Carmencita!

(Entre Carmen.)
(Carmen enters the scene with great panache.)

LES CIGARIÈRES et LES JEUNES GENS
FACTORY GIRLS and YOUNG MEN
La voilà, voilà la Carmencita!
There she is, there she is, Carmencita!

(Elle a un bouquet de cassie à son corsage et une fleur de cassie au coin de la bouche. Des jeunes gens entrent avec Carmen. Ils la suivent, l'entourent, lui parlent. Elle minaude et coquette avec eux. Don José lève la tête. Il regarde Carmen puis se remet tranquillement à travailler.)

(Carmen holds a flower in her mouth. The young men surround her and talk to her, while she flirts with all of them. Don José raises his eyes, looks at Carmen and then continues to work on his chain.)

LES JEUNES GENS
YOUNG MEN
Carmen, sur tes pas nous nous pressons tous;
Carmen, on your steps we hasten all of us;
(Carmen, we hasten to follow your steps;)

Carmen, sois gentille, au moins réponds-nous,
Carmen, be nice, at least answer us,

et dis-nous quel jour tu nous aimeras!
and tell us what day you us will love!

CARMEN
(regardant Don José)
(looking at José)
Quand je vous aimerai? Ma foi, je ne sais pas.
When I you will love? By my faith, I do not know.

Peut-être jamais, peut-être demain;
Maybe never, maybe tomorrow;

mais pas aujourd'hui, c'est certain.
but not today, that's for sure.

NO. 4 HABANERA
NO. 4 HABANERA[5]

CARMEN
L'amour est un oiseau rebelle[6]
Love is a bird rebellious

que nul ne peut apprivoiser,
that nothing not can tame,
(love is a wild bird that nothing can tame,)

et c'est bien en vain qu'on l'appelle,
and it is truly in vain that one calls him,

s'il lui convient de refuser.
if it wants to refuse.

Rien n'y fait, <u>m</u>enace ou prière,
Nothing helps, threats or entreaties,

l'un parle bien, l'autre se tait;
one fellow speaks well, the next one keeps silent;[7]

et c'est l'autre que je préfère,
and it's the other one whom I prefer,

il n'a rien dit, mais il me <u>p</u>laît.
he hasn't anything said but he pleases me.
(Some men talk well, some keep silent, but I prefer the man who says little.)

CHŒUR
CHORUS
L'amour est un oiseau rebelle, etc.

CARMEN
L'amour est enfant de <u>b</u>ohème,
Love is (a) child of bohemia,[8]
(Love is the child of a bohemian's existence,)

il n'a jamais connu de loi.
it hasn't ever known about laws.

Si tu ne m'aimes pas, je t'aime;
If you do not me, I love you;

si je t'aime, prends garde à toi. etc.
if I love you, watch out for yourself. etc.

CARMEN
L'oiseau que tu croyais surprendre
The bird that you thought to surprise

battit de l'aile et s'envola . . .
flapped its wings and flew away . . .

L'amour est loin, tu peux l'attendre;
Love is far away, you can wait for it;

tu ne l'attends plus, il est là.
you don't wait any longer, it is there.

Tout autour de toi, vite, vite,
All around you, quickly, quickly,

il vient, s'en va, puis il revient . . .
it comes, it goes away, then it comes back . . .

Tu crois le tenir, il t'évite,
you think that you have it, it avoids you,

tu crois l'éviter, il te tient.
You think to avoid it, it holds you.

L'amour est enfant de bohème! etc.

NO. 5 SCÈNE
NO. 5 SCENE

LES JEUNES GENS
YOUNG MEN
Carmen! Sur tes pas, nous nous pressons tous!
Carmen! On your steps we hasten all of us!
(Carmen, we hasten to follow your steps!)

Carmen! sois gentille, au moins réponds-nous, etc.
Carmen, be nice, at least answer us, etc.

(Moment de silence. Les jeunes gens entourent Carmen; celle-ci les regarde l'un après l'autre, sort du cercle qu'ils forment autour d'elle et s'en va droit à Don José, qui est toujours occupé avec son épinglette.)
(There is a moment of silence as the young men surround Carmen. She observes them one by one, pushes her way out of the circle they have formed and goes straight towards Don José, who is still quite busy with his saber-pin.)

CARMEN
Eh! Compère, qu'est-ce que tu fais la?
Hey, pal! What are you doing there?

JOSÉ
Je fais une chaîne pour attacher mon épinglette.
I'm making a chain to attach my saber-pin.

CARMEN
Ton épinglette, vraiment! Épinglier de mon âme.
Your saber-pin, really! Saber-pinner of my soul.

(Elle jette une fleur à José. Il se lève brusquement. Il est un rire général. La cloche se met à sonner à nouveau.)
(She throws a flower at José. He rises suddenly. There is general laughter. The bell begins to ring again.)

LES CIGARIÈRES et LES JEUNES GENS
THE GIRLS and YOUNG MEN
L'amour est enfant de bohème, etc.

NO. 5 BIS RÉCITATIVE
NO. 5 BIS RECITATIVE

JOSÉ
Quels regards! Quelle effronterie!
What glances! What brazenness!

Cette fleur-là m'a fait l'effet d'une balle qui m'arrivait!
That flower there had on me the effect of a bullet that was striking me!

Le parfum en est fort et la fleur est jolie.
The perfume of it is strong and the flower is pretty.

Et la femme . . .
And that woman . . .

S'il est vraiment des sorcières,
If there are truly some sorceresses,

c'en est une certainement.
she is one of them, for sure.

MICAËLA
José!

JOSÉ
Micaëla!

MICAËLA
Me voici!
Here I am!

JOSÉ
Quelle joie!
What joy!

MICAËLA
C'est votre mère qui m'envoie.
It's your mother who sends me.

NO. 6 DUO
NO. 6 DUET

JOSÉ
Parle-moi de ma mère.
So speak to me of my mother.

MICAËLA
J'apporte de sa part, fidèle messagère, cette lettre.
I bring from her, faithful messenger, this letter.
(I, as a faithful messenger, bring a letter from her.)

JOSÉ
(en regardant la lettre)
(looking at the letter)

Une lettre!
A letter!

MICAËLA
Et puis un peu d'argent
And also a little money

*(**Elle lui tend un petit sac à main.**)*
(She hands him a small purse.)

pour ajouter à votre traitement, et puis . . .
to add to your salary, and also . . .

JOSÉ
Et puis . . .
And then . . .

MICAËLA
Et puis . . . vraiment je n'ose,
And then . . . truly I do not dare,

et puis encore une autre chose
and then also another thing

qui vaut mieux que l'argent, et qui
that is worth more than money, and which

pour un bon fils aura sans doute plus de prix.
for a good son will have without doubt more value.

JOSÉ
Cette autre chose, quelle est-elle? Parle donc.
That other thing, what is it? Speak then.

MICAËLA
Oui, je parlerai;
Yes, I will speak;

ce que l'on m'a donné je vous le donnerai.
that which she has given I you will give.
(what your mother gave to me I now will give to you.)

Votre mère avec moi sortait de la chapelle,
Your mother with me was leaving the chapel,

et c'est alors qu'en m'embrassant:
and it was then as she embraced me,

"Tu vas," m'a-t'elle dit, "t'en aller à la ville;
"You will," she told me, "go to the town;

la route n'est pas longue, une fois à[9] Séville,
the road is not long, once in Seville,

tu chercheras mon fils, mon José, mon enfant.
you will look for my son, my José, my child.

Et tu lui diras que sa mère
And you to him will tell that his mother

songe nuit et jour à l'absent,
thinks night and day of her absent (son),

qu'elle regrette et qu'elle espère,
that she regrets and that she hopes,

qu'elle pardonne et qu'elle attend.
that she forgives and that she waits.

Tout cela, n'est-ce pas, mignonne,
All of this, not so, my lovely girl,

de ma part tu le lui diras,
from me you to him will say,

et ce baiser que je te donne
and this kiss that I to you give

de ma part tu le lui rendras."
from me you to him will give."

JOSÉ
(très ému)
(very moved)
Un baiser de ma mère!
A kiss from my mother!

MICAËLA
Un baiser pour son fils,
A kiss for her son,

José, je vous le rends, comme je l'ai promis.
José, I to you give it as I have promised.

(Micaëla se hausse un peu sur la pointe des pieds et donne à Don José un baiser bien franc, bien maternel. Don José, très ému, la laisse faire. Il la regarde bien dans les yeux. Un moment de silence.)
(Micaëla rises on her toes and places a maternal kiss on José's forehead. Don José, very moved, lets her proceed, looking tenderly at her all the while.)

JOSÉ
Ma mère, je la vois, oui, je revois mon village.
My mother, I see her, yes, I see again my village.

Ô souvenirs d'autrefois! Doux souvenirs du pays!
Oh memories of other times! Sweet memories of my hometown!

Vous remplissez mon cœur de force et de courage,
You fill my heart with strength and with courage,

ô souvenirs chéris.
oh memories dear.

Ma mère, je la vois, etc.

MICAËLA
Sa **mère,** *il* **la revoit,** etc.
(*He* sees *his* mother, etc.)

Vous remplissez *son* **cœur de force et de courage.** etc.
(You fill *his* heart, etc.)

JOSÉ
(ses yeux fixés sur la manufacture)
(fixing his eyes on the cigarette factory)

Qui sait de quel demon j'allais être la proie!
Who knows of what demon I was about to become the prey!

Même de loin, ma mère me défend,
Even from afar my mother defends me,

et ce baiser qu'elle m'envoie
and that kiss that she sends me

écarte le péril et sauve son enfant.
fends off the danger and saves her son.

MICAËLA
Quel démon? Quel péril? Je ne comprends pas bien.
What demon? What peril? I don't understand quite.

Que veut dire cela?
What means that?

JOSÉ
Rien! Parlons de toi, la messagère.
Nothing! Let us speak about you, the messenger.

Tu vas retourner au pays?
You are going to return to the village?

MICAËLA
Ce soir même, et demain je verrai votre mère.
This evening very, and tomorrow I will see your mother.
(This very evening,)

JOSÉ
Eh bien, tu lui diras
Well then, you her will tell

que son fils l'aime et la vénère,
that her son loves her and worships her,

et qu'il se repent aujourd'hui.
and that he repents today.

Il veut que là-bas sa mère
He wishes that over there his mother

soit contente de lui!
be happy with him!

Tout cela, n'est-ce pas, mignonne,
All that, isn't it so, my pretty one,

de ma part tu le lui diras;
from me you it to her will tell;
(And my pretty one, you will her all that;)

et ce baiser que je te donne,
and this kiss that I give you,

de ma part tu le lui rendras.
from me you it to her will take back.

(Il l'embrasse.)
(He kisses Micaëla.)

MICAËLA
Oui, je vous le promets, de la part de son fils.
Yes, I promise you, on behalf of her son.

José, je le rendrai comme je l'ai promis.
José, I will give it back as I promised.

JOSÉ
Ma mère, je la vois, etc.

MICAËLA
Sa mère, il la revoit, etc.

JOSÉ
Reste là maintenant, pendant que je lirai.
Stay here now, while I read.

MICAËLA
Non pas, lisez d'abord, puis je reviendrai.
Oh no, read first, afterwards I will return.

JOSÉ
Pourquoi t'en aller?
Why do you go away?

MICAËLA
C'est plus sage, cela me convient davantage.
It is wiser, it suits me more.
(It suits me better.)

Lisez, puis je reviendrai.
Read, then I will come back.

JOSÉ
Tu reviendras?
You will come back?

MICAËLA
Je reviendrai.
I will come back.

(Micaëla laisse. José détient la lettre dans sa main et le lit pendant quelques instants.)
(Micaëla leaves. José holds the letter in his hand and reads it for a few moments.)

JOSÉ
Ne crains rien, ma mère, ton fils t'obéira,
Don't fear anything, my mother, your son will obey you,

fera ce que tu lui dis; j'aime Micaëla,
will do all that you tell him; I love Micaëla,

je la prendrai pour femme.
I will take her for my wife.

Quant à tes fleurs, sorcière infâme!
As for your flowers, sorceress vile!
(As for your flowers, Carmen, you vile sorceress!)

NO. 7 CHŒUR
NO. 7 CHORUS

(Au moment où il va arracher la fleur de sa veste, grande rumeur dans l'intérieur de la manufacture. Entre Zuniga suivi des soldats.)
(At the very moment when he is about to throw the flower away, a loud noise is heard coming from inside the factory. Zuniga enters, followed by soldiers.)

ZUNIGA
Que se passe-t-il donc là-bas?
What is happening then over there?

GROUPE DE FEMMES
CHORUS WOMEN
Au secours! N'entendez-vous pas? Au secours messieurs les soldats!
Help! Can't you hear? Help, (mister) soldiers!

PREMIER GROUPE DE FEMMES
FIRST GROUP OF WOMEN
C'est la Carmencita!
It's Carmencita!

DEUXIÈME GROUPE DE FEMMES
SECOND GROUP OF WOMEN
Non, non, ce n'est pas elle!
No, no, it isn't she!

PREMIER GROUPE DE FEMMES
FIRST GROUP OF WOMEN
C'est elle.
It's she.

DEUXIÈME GROUPE DE FEMMES
SECOND GROUP OF WOMEN
Pas du tout.
Not at all.

PREMIER GROUPE DE FEMMES
FIRST GROUP OF WOMEN
Si fait! C'est elle!
For sure! It's she!

Elle a porté les premiers coups.
She did strike the first blows.

TOUTES LES FEMMES
ALL WOMEN
(entourant Zuniga)
(surrounding Zuniga)
Ne les écoutez pas, monsieur, écoutez-nous.
Don't them listen to, sir, listen to us.

PREMIER GROUPE DE FEMMES
FIRST GROUP OF WOMEN
(tirant sur Zuniga)
(pulling at Zuniga)
La Manuelita disait et répétait à voix haute
Manuelita said and repeated in a loud voice

qu'elle achèterait sans faute
that she would buy without fault

un âne qui lui plaisait.
an ass that her would please.

DEUXIÈME GROUPE DE FEMMES
SECOND GROUP OF WOMEN
(faire la même chose)
(doing the same)
Alors la Carmencita, railleuse à son ordinaire,
Then Carmencita, mocking as is her custom,

dit: "Un âne, pourquoi faire?
said: "An ass, whatever for?

Un balai te suffira."
A broom will do for you."

PREMIER GROUPE DE FEMMES
FIRST GROUP OF WOMEN
Manuelita riposta, et dit à sa camarade:
Manuelita retorted and said to her friend:

"Pour certaine promenade mon âne te servira.
"For a certain ride my donkey will be of use to you.[10]

DEUXIÈME GROUPE DE FEMMES
SECOND GROUP OF WOMEN
Et ce jour-là tu pourras à bon droit faire la fière
And on that day you can in your own right play the proud lady

deux laquais suivront derrière,
two lackeys will follow behind,

t'émouchant à tour de bras."
keeping flies off you by waving their arms."

TOUTES LES FEMMES
ALL WOMEN
Là-dessus toutes les deux
There all two of them

se sont prises[11] aux cheveux.
they each other pulled at their hairs.
(they began to grab each other by the hair.)

ZUNIGA
Au diable tout ce bavardage!
To the devil (with) all this chatter!

(pour José)
(to José)

Prenez, José, deux hommes avec vous
Take, José, two men with you

et voyez là-dedans qui cause ce tapage.
and see inside who causes that commotion.

(Don José prend deux hommes avec lui. Les soldats rentrent dans la manufacture. Pendant ce temps les femmes se pressent, se disputent entre elles.)
(José takes two men with him. Meanwhile the women continue to fight and push.)

PREMIER GROUPE DE FEMMES
FIRST GROUP OF WOMEN
C'est la Carmencita!
It's Carmencita!

Rosa Ponselle as Carmen, 1936

Robert Merrill as Escamillo, 1946
METROPOLITAN OPERA ARCHIVES

Risë Stevens as Carmen, 1952
Bender / Metropolitan Opera Archives

Risë Stevens as Carmen and Richard Tucker as Don José
in Tyrone Guthrie's landmark production, 1952

Two scenes from the 1967–68 production, with Grace
Bumbry as Carmen, Nicolai Gedda as Don José, and
Justino Díaz as Escamillo

Shirley Verrett as Carmen and Jon Vickers as Don José, 1968

Regina Resnik as Carmen and James King as Don José, 1968 (top)
Marilyn Horne as Carmen, 1972 (bottom)
METROPOLITAN OPERA ARCHIVES

Régine Crespin as Carmen, 1975
ERIKA DAVIDSON / METROPOLITAN OPERA ARCHIVES

DEUXIÈME GROUPE DE FEMMES
SECOND GROUP OF WOMEN
Non, non, écoutez-nous, etc.
No, no, listen to us, etc.

ZUNIGA
(assourdi par le vacarme)
(deafened by the racket)
Holà! Éloignez-moi toutes ces femmes-là.
Hey there! Rid me of all those women.

TOUTES LES FEMMES
ALL WOMEN
Écoutez-nous!
Listen to us!

(Les soldats repoussent les femmes et les écartent.)
(The soldiers push off the women and force them to disperse.)

NO. 8 CHANSON ET LE MÈLODRAME
NO. 8 SONG AND MELODRAMA

(Carmen paraît sur la porte de la manufacture amenée par Don José et suivie par deux dragons.)
(Carmen appears at the door of the factory, held by Don José and followed by some dragoons.)

JOSÉ
Mon officier, c'était une querelle;
Sir, it was a quarrel;

des injures d'abord, puis à la fin des coups,
some insults at first, then at the end some blows,

une femme blessée.
a woman wounded.

ZUNIGA
Et par qui?
And by wohm?

JOSÉ
Mais par elle.
Why, by her.

ZUNIGA
Vous entendez, que nous répondrez-vous?
You have heard, what have you to say to us?

CARMEN
Tra la la, ҫoupe-moi, b̲rûle-moi, je ne te dirai rien;
Tra la la, beat me, burn me, I won't tell you anything;

tra la la, je brave tout, le feu,
tra la la I defy everything, fire,

le fer, et le ciel même!
the iron,[12] and heaven itself!

ZUNIGA
Fais-nous grâce de tes chansons,
Spare us of your songs,

et puisque l'on t'a dit de répondre, r̲éponds!
And since we told you to answer, a̲nswer!

CARMEN
Tra la, mon secret je le garde et je le garde b̲ien.
Tra la, my secret I keep and I keep it well.

Tra la, j'en aime un autre et je meurs en disant que je l'aime.
Tra la, I love another and I die as I say that I love him.

ZUNIGA
Puisque tu le prends sur ce ton,
Since you take on that attitude,

tu chanteras ton air aux murs de la prison.
you can sing your song to the walls of the prison.

FILLES DE CIGARETTES
CIGARETTE GIRLS

En prison!
To prison!

(Carmen veut se précipiter sur les femmes, même en essayant de mordre la main de Zuniga.)
(Carmen hurls herself on the cigarette girls, even trying to bite Zuniga's hand.)

ZUNIGA
La peste! Décidément vous avez la main leste!
The pest on you! Decidedly you have a hand quick!

CARMEN
Tra la la . . .

ZUNIGA
C'est dommage, c'est grand dommage,
It's a shame, it's a big shame,

car elle est gentille vraiment!
for she is nice, really!

Mais il faut bien la rendre sage,
But we must make her be well-behaved,

attachez ces deux jolis bras.
bind those two pretty arms.

(Exit Zuniga. Un petit moment de silence. Carmen lève les yeux et regarde Don José. Celui-ci se détourne, s'éloigne de quelques pas, puis revient à Carmen qui le regarde toujours.)
(There is a moment of silence. José puts a rope around Carmen's wrists. The crowd gradually disperses.)

CARMEN
Où me conduirez-vous?
Where are you taking me?

JOSÉ
À la prison et je n'y puis rien faire.
To prison and I cannot about it nothing do.

CARMEN
Vraiment? Tu n'y peux rien faire?
Really? You cannot about it nothing do?

JOSÉ
Non, rien! J'obéis à mes chefs.
No, nothing! I obey (to) my superiors.

CARMEN
Eh bien, moi, je sais bien qu'en dépit
Ah well, me, I know full well that in spite

de tes chefs eux-mêmes[13]
of your superiors themselves

tu feras tout ce que je veux,
you will do everything that I want,

et cela parce que tu m'aimes.
and that because you love me.

JOSÉ
Moi, t'aimer?
I, love you?

CARMEN
Oui, José. La fleur dont je t'ai fait présent,
Yes, José. The flower of which I made you a gift,

tu sais, la fleur de la sorcière,
you know, the flower of the sorceress,

tu peux la jeter maintenant, le charme opère.
you can throw it away now, the spell is working.

JOSÉ
Ne me parle plus! Tu m'entends!
Don't speak to me anymore! You understand me!

Ne parle plus. Je le <u>d</u>éfends!
Don't speak anymore. I forbid it!

NO. 9 SÉGUEDILLE ET DUO
NO. 9 SEGIDILLA AND DUET

CARMEN
Près des remparts de Séville,
Near the ramparts of Seville,

chez mon ami Lillas Pastia,
at my friend Lillas Pastia,

j'irai danser la séguedille et boire du Manzanilla! . . . [14]
I will dance the seguidilla and drink some Manzanilla . . .

Oui, mais toute seule on s'ennuie,
Yes, but all alone one gets bored,

et les vrais plaisirs sont à deux . . .
and the true pleasures are for two . . .
(and true pleasure should be shared . . .)

donc,[15] **pour me tenir compagnie, j'emmènerai mon amoureux.**
therefore, to keep me company, I will take my lover.

Mon amoureux! . . . Il est au diable . . .
My lover! . . . He has gone to the devil . . .

je l'ai mis à la porte hier . . .
I threw him out the door yesterday . . .

Mon pauvre cœur très consolable,
My poor heart very consolable,

mon cœur est libre comme l'air . . .
my heart is free like the air . . .

J'ai des galants à la douzaine
I have (some) lovers by the dozen

mais ils ne sont pas à mon gré.
but they are not to my liking.

Voici la fin de la semaine,
Here is the end of the week,
(Here comes the weekend,)

qui veut m'aimer, je l'aimerai,
whoever wants to love me, I will love him,

qui veut mon âme? Elle est à prendre,
whoever wants my soul, it is for the taking,

vous arrivez au bon moment.
you are arriving at the (right) moment.

Je n'ai guère le temps d'attendre,
I don't have hardly the time to wait,

car avec mon nouvel amant . . .
for with my new lover . . .

Près des remparts de Séville, chez mon ami Lillas Pastia, etc.

JOSÉ
Tais-toi, je t'avais dit de ne pas me parler!
Be quiet, I told you not to talk to me!

CARMEN
Je ne te parle pas, je chante pour moi-même
I am not talking, I am singing to myself

et je pense . . . il n'est pas défendu de penser,
and I was thinking . . . it isn't forbidden to think,

je pense à certain[16] officier,
I am thinking of a certain officer,

qui m'aime, et qu'à mon tour je pourrais bien aimer.
who loves me, and whom at my turn I could really love.

JOSÉ
(perdre lentement son emprise)
(slowly losing his grip)
Carmen! . . .

CARMEN
Mon officier n'est pas un capitaine,
My officer is not a captain,

pas même un lieutenant, il n'est que brigadier:
not even a lieutenant, he isn't but a corporal:

mais c'est assez pour une bohémienne,
but it is enough for a gypsy girl,

et je daigne m'en contenter!
and I deign to content myself with him!

JOSÉ
(déliant la corde qui attache les mains de Carmen)
(as he unties the rope around her wrists)
Carmen, je suis comme un homme ivre,
Carmen, I am like a man drunk,
(Carmen, I feel like a drunken man,)

si je cède, si je me livre,
if I give in, if I can get free,

ta promesse, tu la tiendras,
your promise, you will keep it,

si je t'aime, tu m'aimeras . . .
if I love you, you will love me . . .

CARMEN
Oui . . . nous danserons la séguedille en buvant du manzanilla . . .
Yes, we will dance the seguidilla . . . while drinking some
manzanilla . . .

JOSÉ
(chuchotant tout en la tenant)
(whispering while holding her)
Chez Lillas Pastia . . . tu le promets . . . Carmen . . .
At Lillas Pastia's . . . you promise . . . Carmen . . .

CARMEN
Ah! Près des remparts de Séville, etc.

JOSÉ
Nous danserons la séguedilla et boirons du manzanilla.
We will dance the seguidilla and will drink some manzanilla.

NO. 10 FINALE
NO. 10 FINALE

ZUNIGA
Voici l'ordre, partez, et faites bonne garde.
Here's the order, leave, and keep a good lookout.

CARMEN
(bas à José)
(in a low voice to José)
Sur le chemin je te pousserai
On the way I will push you

aussi fort que je le pourrai . . .
as hard as I can do it . . .

laisse-toi renverser . . . le reste me regarde.
allow yourself to fall over . . . the rest is up to me.

(Elle se place entre les deux dragons. José à côté d'elle. Les femmes et les bourgeois pendant ce temps sont rentrés en scène, toujours maintenus à distance par les dragons. Carmen traverse la scène allant vers le pont.)
(Carmen begins to leave, followed by José, who pretends to be holding her wrists.)

L'amour est enfant de bohème, etc.
(En arrivant à l'entrée du pont, Carmen pousse José qui se laisse renverser. Confusion, désordre, Carmen s'enfuit. Arrivée au milieu du pont, elle s'arrête un instant, jette sa corde à la volée par-dessus le parapet du pont, et se sauve pendant qu'à la scène, avec de grands éclats de rire, les cigarières entourent Zuniga.)
(Once arrived at the proper place, Carmen pushes José, who falls down, allowing her to escape. There is a great commotion as the cigarette girls express their joy. Zuniga has the dragoons arrest José, who is taken off to prison.)

FIN DE L'ACTE I
END OF ACT I

DEUXIÈME ACTE
ACT II

(La taverne de Lillas Pastia, Carmen, Mercédès, Frasquita, le lieu-tenant Zuniga, Moralès et un lieutenant. C'est la fin d'un dîner. La table est en désordre. Les officiers et les bohémiennes fument des cigarettes. Deux bohémiens râclent de la guitare dans un coin de la taverne et deux bohémiennes, au milieu de la scène, dansent. Carmen est assise, regardant danser les bohémiennes. Un officier lui parle bas, mais elle ne fait aucune attention à lui. Elle se lève tout à coup et se met à chanter.)

(Inside Lillas Pastia's tavern, Zuniga, Moralès, Carmen, Fraquita and Mercédès are milling about the crowd of customers, soldiers, gypsies and dancers. Some are smoking, some drinking and some playing cards.)

NO. 11 CHANSON BOHÈME
NO. 11 GYPSY SONG

CARMEN
Les tringles des sistres tintaient,
The rods of the sistrums[1] jingled,

avec un éclat métallique,
with a clatter metallic,

et sur cette étrange musique
and on that strange music

les zingarellas se levaient.
the gypsy girls stood up.

Tambours de basque allaient leur train,
Tambourines kept their beat,
(Tambourines were keeping time,)

et les guitares forcenées
and the guitars frenzied

grinçaient sous des mains obstinées
ground away under hands persistent

même chanson, même refrain.
(the) same song, (the) same refrain.

Les anneaux de cuivre et d'argent,
The rings of copper and silver,

reluisaient sur les peaux bistrées;
shone on skins swarthy;

d'orange ou de rouge zébrées
with orange or with red stripes[2]

les étoffes flottaient au vent.
the dress fabrics floated in the wind.

La danse au chant se mariait,
The dance to the song were married,
(Dance and song became as one,)

d'abord indécise et timide,
at first timid and hesitant,

plus vive ensuite et plus rapide,
more lively then and more rapid,

cela montait, montait! . . .
it grew, (and) grew! . . .

Les bohémiens à tour de bras,
The gypsies, with all their strength,

de leurs instruments faisaient rage,[3]
of their instruments made rage,
(they played away [as possessed by a rage] on their instruments,)

et cet éblouissant tapage,
and this deafening uproar,

ensorcelait les zingaras!
bewitched the gypsy girls!

Sous le rythme de la chanson,
Under the rhythm of the song,

ardentes, folles, enfiévrées,
ardent, mad, feverish,

elles se laissaient, enivrées,
they allowed themselves, intoxicated,

emporter par le tourbillon!
(to be) carried away by the whirl!

(La danse prend de la vitesse comme les zingaras, Carmen, Frasquita et Mercédès rejoindre dans le tournoiement danse, au milieu des cris d'approbation des autres.)
(The dance picks up speed as the gypsies, Carmen, Frasquita and Mercédès join in the whirling dancing, amid shouts of approbation from the others.)

NO. 12 BIS RÉCITATIVE
NO. 12 BIS RECITATIVE

FRASQUITA
Messieurs, Pastia me dit . . .
Gentlemen, Pastia told me . . .

ZUNIGA
Que nous veut-il encore, maître Pastia?
What does he want from us again, master Pastia?

FRASQUITA
Il dit que le Corrégidor[4] veut que l'on ferme l'auberge.
He says that the *corregidor* wants that we shut down the inn.

ZUNIGA
Eh bien! Nous partirons. Vous viendrez avec nous?
Ah well! We will go. You will come with us?

FRASQUITA
Non pas! Nous, nous restons.
Not at all! We . . . we will stay (here).

ZUNIGA
Et toi, Carmen, tu ne viens pas?
And you, Carmen, you aren't coming?

Écoute! Deux mots dits tout bas: tu m'en veux.
Listen, two words said very softly: you dislike me.

CARMEN
Vous en vouloir! Pourquoi?
You dislike! Why?

ZUNIGA
Ce soldat, l'autre jour, emprisonné pour toi.
That soldier, the other day, sent to prison on account of you.

CARMEN
Qu'a-t-on fait de ce malheureux?
What did they do with that unfortunate man?

ZUNIGA
Maintenant il est libre.
Now he is free.
(Now he is out free from jail.)

CARMEN
Il est libre, tant mieux.
He is free, so much the better.

Bonsoir, messieurs nos amoureux!
Good night, gentlemen our swains!
(Good night to our gentlemen admirers!)

FRASQUITA et MERCÉDÈS
Bonsoir, messieurs nos amoureux!

(Le son d'un chœur d'animation se fait entendre dans les coulisses.)
(The sound of an animated chorus is heard offstage.)

NO. 13 CHŒUR
NO. 13 CHORUS
Vivat⁵ le Toréro! Vivat Escamillo!
Long live the bullfighter! Long live Escamillo!

ZUNIGA
Une promenade aux flambeaux!
A parade of torches!
(A torchlight parade)

C'est le vainqueur des courses de Grenade.
It's the winner of the bullfights in Granada.

Voulez-vous avec nous boire, mon camarade,
Do you want to with us drink, my friend,

à vos succès anciens, à vos succès nouveaux!
to your triumphs past (and) to your triumphs new!

CHŒUR
CHORUS
Vivat le Toréro, etc.

(Il s'agit d'une réaction forte de tout le monde et Escamillo apparaît.
Pastia lui apporte un verre et les filles, tout excité à la vue du beau
matador, afficher leurs meilleurs côtés soient correctement admirés.)
(There is a loud reaction from everyone and Escamillo appears. Pastia brings
him a drink and the girls, all excited at the sight of the handsome matador,
display their best sides to be properly admired.)

NO. 13 COUPLETS (CHANSON DU TORÉRO)
NO. 13 COUPLETS (TORÉADOR⁶ SONG⁷)

Votre toast, je peux vous le rendre,
Your toast, I can return to you,

señors, car avec les soldats,
gentlemen, for with the soldiers,

oui, les toréros peuvent s'entendre,
yes, the *toreros* can understand one another,

pour plaisirs ils ont les combats!
for pleasure they have their fights!
(fighting is their game!)

Le cirque est plein, c'est jour de fête,
The arena is full, it is a day of *fiesta*,

le cirque est plein du haut en bas.
the arena is full from top to bottom.

Les spectateurs perdant la tête,
The spectators, losing their wits,

les spectateurs s'interpellent à grand fracas.
the spectators yell at one another with great racket.
(yell at each other at the top of their lungs.)

Apostrophes, cris et tapage
Exclamations, yells and uproar

poussés jusques à la fureur!
carried to a furor!

Car c'est la fête du courage!
For it is the fiesta of courage!

C'est la fête des gens de cœur!
It is the fiesta of people stout-hearted!

Allons! En garde, allons, ah!
Let's go, on your guard, let's go, ah!

Toréador, en garde!
Bullfighter, on (your) guard!

Et songe bien, oui songe en combattant
And think well, yes think while you're fighting

qu'un œil noir te regarde et que l'amour t'attend.
that an eye black watches you and that love awaits you.
(that a woman's black eyes are watching you and that love awaits you.)

TOUT LE MONDE
ALL
Toréador, en garde, etc.

ESCAMILLO
Tout d'un coup, on fait silence . . . ah, que se passe-t-il?
All of a sudden, they are silent . . . ah, what is happening?

Plus de cris, c'est l'instant!
No more shouts, it's the moment!

Le taureau s'élance en bondissant hors du Toril!
The bull hurls itself, bounding out of the Toril![8]

Il s'élance! Il entre, il frappe,
It charges, it enters, it strikes,

un cheval roule, entraînant un picador,
a horse rolls over, dragging down a picador,

"Ah bravo Toro!" hurle la foule,
"Ah brave bull," shouts the crowd,

le taureau va . . . il vient . . . et frappe encor!
the bull goes . . . it comes (back) . . . and strikes again!

En secouant ses banderilles, plein de fureur il court!
Shaking its banderillas,[9] full of fury it runs!
([Trying to] shake off the banderillas, he runs [around] full of fury!)

Le cirque est plein de sang!
The arena is full of blood!

On se sauve . . . on franchit les grilles!
Men leap clear . . . the bound over the barriers!

C'est ton tour maintenant!
It's your turn now!

Toréador, en garde, etc.

TOUT LE MONDE
CHORUS
Toréador, en garde, etc.

NO. 14a RÉCITATIVE
NO. 14a RECITATIVE

ESCAMILLO
(aller sur Carmen)
(going over to Carmen)
La belle, un mot:
You pretty one, one word:

comment t'appelle-t-on? Dans mon premier danger
what do they call you? At my first danger

je veux dire ton nom.
I want to say your name.
(At the time of my worst danger I wish to utter your name.)

CARMEN
Carmen, Carmencita, cela revient au même.
Carmen, Carmencita, it comes to the same thing.
(Carmen or Carmencita, it's all the same.)

ESCAMILLO
Si l'on te disait que l'on t'aime?
If someone were to say that he loves you?

CARMEN
Je répondrais qu'il ne faut pas m'aimer.
I would reply that one should not love me.

ESCAMILLO
Cette réponse n'est pas tendre;
That answer is not friendly;

je me contenterai d'espérer et d'attendre.
I will content myself with hoping and with waiting.

CARMEN
Il est permis d'attendre, il est doux d'espérer.
It is permitted to wait, it is sweet to hope.

ZUNIGA
Puisque tu ne viens pas, Carmen, je reviendrai.
Since you aren't coming, Carmen, I will return.

CARMEN
Et vous aurez grand tort.
And you will be very wrong.
(And you will be making a big mistake.)

ZUNIGA
Bah! Je me risquerai!
Bah! I will take my chances!

(Escamillo sort, suivi par ses admirateurs. Il jette un regard significatif à Carmen avant de sortir.)
(Escamillo exits, followed by his admirers. He casts a meaningful glance at Carmen before going out.)

NO. 14b RÉCITATIVE
NO. 14b RECITATIVE

FRASQUITA
Eh! Bien! Vite, quelles nouvelles?
Hey! Well? Quickly, what news?

LE DANCAÏRE
DANCAIRO
Pas trop mauvaises les nouvelles,
Not too bad, the news,

et nous pouvons encore faire quelques beaux coups!
and we can still pull off some lovely jobs!

Mais nous avons besoin de vous.
But we are in need of you.
(But we need your help.)

FRASQUITA, MERCÉDÈS et CARMEN
Besoin de nous?
Need of us?

LE DANCAÏRE
DANCAIRO
Oui, nous avons besoin de vous.
Yes, we are in need of you.

NO. 15 QUINTETTE
NO. 15 QUINTET

LE DANCAÏRE
DANCAIRO
Nous avons en tête une affaire.
We have in mind a job.

MERCÉDÈS
Est-elle bonne, dites-nous?
Is it (a) good one, tell us?

LE DANCAÏRE
DANCAIRO
Elle est admirable, ma chère;
It is admirable, my dear;

mais nous avons besoin de vous.
but we have need of you.

LES TROIS FEMMES
THE THREE WOMEN
De nous?
Of us?

LE DANCAÏRE et LE REMENDADO
DANCAIRO and REMENDADO
De vous, car nous l'avouons humblement
Of you, for we admit it humbly

et fort respectueusement.
and quite respectfully.

Quand il[10] s'agit de tromperie,[11] de duperie, de volerie,
When it's a matter of trickery, of deceit, of thievery,

il est toujours bon, sur ma foi,
it is always good, upon my faith,

d'avoir les femmes avec soi,
having the women with us,

et sans elles, mes toutes belles,
and without them, my beautiful ones,

on ne fait jamais rien de bien.
we don't do never nothing well.
(we never do anything well.)

FRASQUITA, MERCÉDÈS et CARMEN
Quoi! Sans nous jamais rien de bien?
What! Without us never anything well?

LE DANCAÏRE et LE REMENDADO
DANCAIRO and REMENDADO
N'êtes-vous pas de cet avis.
Aren't you not of that opinion.

FRASQUITA, MERCÉDÈS et CARMEN
Si fait, je suis de cet avis.
Indeed, I am of that opinion.

TOUS LES CINQ
ALL FIVE
Quand il s'agit de tromperie, etc.[12]

LE DANCAÏRE
DANCAIRO
C'est dit alors, vous partirez.
It's settled then, you will go.

FRASQUITA et MERCÉDÈS
Quand vous voudrez.
Whenever you wish.

LE DANCAÏRE
DANCAIRO
Mais tout de suite.
But immediately.

CARMEN
(pour Mercédès et Frasquita)
(to Mercédès and Frasquita)
Ah! Permettez. S'il vous plaît de partir, partez,
Ah! Allow me. If it pleases you to go, go,

mais je ne suis pas du voyage.
but I am not for (this) trip.

Je ne pars pas!
I am not going!

LE DANCAÏRE et LE REMENDADO
DANCAIRO and REMENDADO
Carmen, mon amour, tu viendras,
Carmen, my love, you will come,

et tu n'auras pas le courage
and you won't have the heart

de nous laisser dans l'embarras.
of us leaving in the lurch.
(and you won't have the heart to leave us in the lurch.)

CARMEN
Je ne pars pas!
I am not going!

LE DANCAÏRE
DANCAIRO
Mais au moins la raison, Carmen, tu la diras?
But at least the reason, Carmen, you will tell us?

CARMEN
Je la dirai certainement.
I will tell you, certainly.

DANCAIRO, REMENDADO, FRASQUITA, MERCÉDÈS
Voyons!
Let's hear it!

CARMEN
La raison, c'est qu'en ce moment . . .
The reason is that at this moment . . .

TOUS LES QUATRE
ALL FOUR
Eh bien?
Well? . . .

CARMEN
Je suis amoureuse.
I am in love.

LE DANCAÏRE et LE REMENDADO
DANCAIRO and REMENDADO
(stupéfaits)
(amazed)
Qu'a-t-elle dit?
What did she say?

FRASQUITA et MERCÉDÈS
Elle dit qu'elle est amoureuse!
She says that she is in love!

TOUS LES QUATRE
ALL FOUR
Amoureuse!
In love!

CARMEN
Oui, amoureuse!
Yes, in love!

LE DANCAÏRE
DANCAIRO
Voyons, Carmen, sois sérieuse.
See here, Carmen, be serious.

CARMEN
Amoureuse à perdre l'esprit!
In love up to losing my senses!
(I am head over heels in love!)

LE DANCAÏRE et LE REMENDADO
DANCAIRO, REMENDADO
La chose certes nous étonne,
The matter surely astounds us,

mais ce n'est pas le premier jour
but it is not the first time

où vous aurez su, ma mignonne,
where you will have known, my pretty,

faire marcher de front le devoir et l'amour.
to make walk ahead the duty and love.
(It's not the first time that you went ahead and combined duty and love.)

CARMEN
Mes amis, je serais fort aise
My friends, I would be most happy

de partir avec vous ce soir
to leave with you this evening

mais cette fois, ne vous déplaise,
but this time may, it not displease you,

il faudra que l'amour passe avant le devoir.
it is necessary that love go before the duty.

LE DANCAÏRE
DANCAIRO
Ce n'est pas là ton dernier mot?
Is it not that your last word?
(Is that your final word?)

CARMEN
Absolument!
Absolutely!

LE REMENDADO
REMENDADO
Il faut que tu te laisses attendrir.
It is necessary that you allow yourself to be softened.
(You must relent.)

TOUS LES QUATRE
ALL FOUR
Il faut venir, Carmen, pour notre affaire,
You must come, Carmen, (for the sake of) our job,

c'est nécessaire, car entre nous . . .
it is necessary, for between ourselves . . .

CARMEN
Quant à cela, je l'admets avec vous . . .
As far as that, I admit it with you . . .

TOUS LES CINQ
ALL FIVE
Quand il s'agit de tromperie, etc.

LE DANCAÏRE
DANCAIRO
Mais qui donc attends-tu?
But who then awaits you?
(Whom are you waiting for?)

CARMEN
Presque rien, un soldat qui l'autre jour
Almost nothing, a soldier who the other day

pour me rendre service
to do me a favor

s'est fait mettre en prison.
had himself put in prison.
(Nothing much. Just some soldier who the other day got himself thrown into jail for doing me a favor.)

LE REMENDADO
REMENDADO
Le fait est délicat.
The situation is delicate.

LE DANCAÏRE
DANCAIRO
Il se peut qu'après tout ton soldat réfléchisse.
It is possible that after all your soldier changed his mind.

Es-tu bien sûre qu'il viendra?
Are you quite sure that he will come?

NO. 16 CHANSON
NO. 16 SONG

JOSÉ
Halte là! Qui va là? Dragon d'Alcalá!
Halt! Who goes there? Dragoon of Alcalá! [13]

CARMEN
Écoutez!
Listen!

JOSÉ
Où t'en vas-tu par là, Dragon d'Alcalá?
Where are you going over there, Dragoon of Alcalá?

CARMEN
Le voilà!
There he is!

JOSÉ
Moi, je m'en vais faire mordre la poussière
I, I am going to make bite the dust

à mon adversaire.
to my rival.
(I am going to make my rival bite the dust.)

S'il en est ainsi, passez, mon ami.
If it is like that, pass, my friend.

Affaire d'honneur, affaire de cœur,
A matter of honor, an affair of the heart,

pour nous tout est là, dragons d'Alcalá!
for us all is clear, dragoons of Alcala!

FRASQUITA
C'est un beau dragon!
He is a handsome dragoon!

MERCÉDÈS
Un très beau dragon!
A very handsome dragoon!

LE DANCAÏRE
DANCAIRO
Qui serait pour nous un fier compagnon.
Who would be for us a proud companion.

LE REMENDADO
REMENDADO
Dis-lui de nous suivre.
Tell him to come with us.

CARMEN
Il refusera.
He will refuse.

LE DANCAÏRE
DANCAIRO
Mais essaye, au moins.
But try, at least.

CARMEN
Soit! On essayera.
So be it! I will try.

JOSÉ
(la voix beaucoup plus rapprochée)
(the sound of his voice much nearer this time)
Halte là, Dragon d'Alcalá! etc.

Exact et fidèle je vais où m'appelle
Punctual and faithful I go where it calls me

l'amour de ma belle!
the love of my sweetheart!

S'il en est ainsi, passez, mon ami, etc.

NO. 16 BIS RÉCITATIVE
NO. 16 BIS RECITATIVE

CARMEN
Enfin, c'est toi!
Finally, it's you!

JOSÉ
Carmen!

CARMEN
Et tu sors de prison?
And you (just) came out of jail?

JOSÉ
J'y suis resté deux mois.
I did there stay two months.

CARMEN
Tu t'en plains?
You are about it complaining?

JOSÉ
Ma foi, non!
By my faith, no!

Et si c'était pour toi, j'y voudrais être encore.
And if it were for you, I there would like to be still.
(And if it were for you, I'd gladly be there still.)

CARMEN
Tu m'aimes donc?[14]
You love me, then?

JOSÉ
Je t'adore!
I adore you!

CARMEN
Vos officiers sont venus tout à l'heure,
Your officers came here just now,

ils nous ont fait danser.
they made us dance.

JOSÉ
Comment? Toi?
How so? You?

CARMEN
Que je meure si tu n'es pas jaloux!
May I die if you aren't jealous!

JOSÉ
Eh oui, je suis jaloux.
Hey yes, I am jealous.
(I'm jealous all right!)

NO. 17 DUO
NO. 17 DUET

CARMEN
Tout doux, monsieur, tout doux,
Easy, mister, easy does it,

je vais danser en votre honneur,
I am going to dance in your honor,

et vous verrez, Seigneur,
and you will see, sir,

comment je sais moi-même accompagner ma danse.
how I know myself to accompany my dancing.

Mettez-vous là, Don José, je commence.
Sit yourself there, Don José, I am starting.

(Elle fait asseoir Don José dans un coin du théâtre. Petite danse, Carmen, du bout des lèvres, fredonne un air qu'elle accompagne avec ses castagnettes. Don José la dévore des yeux. On entend au loin des clairons qui sonnent la retraite. Don José prête l'oreille. Il s'approche de Carmen, et l'oblige à arrêter.)
(She makes José sit down and sings and dances, accompanying herself with castanets. José is totally entranced. Bugles are heard in the distance sounding the retreat for return to camp. José listens and immediately comes over to Carmen, begging her to stop.)

JOSÉ
Attends un peu, Carmen, rien qu'un moment, arrête.
Wait a bit, Carmen, but one moment, stop.

CARMEN
Et pourquoi, s'il te plaît?
And why, if you please?

JOSÉ
Il me semble, là-bas . . . oui, ce sont nos clairons
It seems to me, over there . . . yes, it is our bugles

qui sonnent la retraite, ne les entends-tu pas?
that are sounding the retreat, can't you hear them?

CARMEN
Bravo! J'avais beau faire . . . il est mélancolique de danser sans orchestre.
Bravo! I was trying in vain . . . it is depressing to dance without orchestra.

Et vive la musique qui nous tombe du ciel!
And hurrah (for) the music that to us falls from heaven!

(Elle reprend sa chanson. La retraite approche, passe sous les fenêtres de l'auberge, puis s'éloigne.)
(She continues her singing and dancing. The bugles get louder and louder. There is a new effort by José to stop watching Carmen.)

JOSÉ
Tu ne m'as pas compris . . . Carmen, c'est la retraite . . .
You haven't understood . . . Carmen, it's the retreat . . .

il faut que moi, je rentre au quartier pour l'appel.
It is necessary that I, I return to the barracls for roll-call.

CARMEN
(stupéfait)
(stupefied)
Au quartier! Pour l'appel!
To the barracks! For roll-call!

Ah! J'étais vraiment trop bête!
Ah! I was in truth too stupid!

Je me mettais en quatre[15] et je faisais des frais
I went out of my way and I took the trouble

pour amuser monsieur!
to amuse *monsieur*!

Je chantais! Je dansais! Je crois, Dieu me pardonne,
I sang! I danced! I think, God forgive me,

qu'un peu plus, je l'aimais! Taratata!
that in a while more I would love him! Taratata!

C'est le clairon qui sonne!
It's the bugle that is sounding!

Taratata! Il part, il est parti!
Taratata! He leaves, he is gone!

Va-t'en donc, canari! Tiens! Prends ton shako,
Leave then, canary![16] Here! Take your cap,

ton sabre, ta giberne;
your saber, your bandolier;

et va-t'en, mon garçon, retourne à ta caserne!
so leave here, my boy, return to your barracks!

JOSÉ
C'est mal à toi, Carmen, de te moquer de moi;
It's wrong of you, Carmen, to make fun of me;

je souffre de partir, car jamais femme,
I suffer in leaving, for never a woman,

jamais femme avant toi,
never a woman before you,

aussi profondément n'avait troublé mon âme!
so profoundly has troubled my soul!

CARMEN[17]
Il souffre de partir, car jamais, jamais femme, jamais femme avant moi aussi profondément n'avait troublé son âme.
Taratata, mon Dieu! C'est la retraite!
Taratata, my God! It's the retreat!

Taratata, je vais être en retard!
Taratata, I will be late!

Il perd la tête, il court, et voilà son amour!
He loses his head, he runs, and there is his love!

JOSÉ
Ainsi, tu ne crois pas à mon amour?
So, you don't believe in my love?

CARMEN
Mais non!
Of course not!

JOSÉ
Eh bien! Tu m'entendras!
Very well! You will hear me out!

CARMEN
Je ne veux rien entendre!
I don't want nothing to hear!

JOSÉ
Tu m'entendras!

CARMEN
Tu vas te faire attendre!
You will make yourself wait!
(It's going to cause them to wait for you!)
(You're going to be late!)

JOSÉ
Tu m'entendras!

CARMEN
Non, non!

JOSÉ
Oui, tu m'entendras!

Je le veux, Carmen, tu m'entendras!
I want it, Carmen, you will hear me out!

ARIA—CHANSON DE FLEUR
ARIA—FLOWER SONG

La fleur que tu m'avais jetée,
The flower that you at did me throw,

dans ma prison m'était restée.
in my prison with me stayed.

Flétrie et sèche, cette fleur
Withered and dried up, that flower

gardait toujours sa <u>d</u>ouce odeur;
kept always its sweet fragrance;

et pendant des heures entières,
and during the hours entire,
(and for entire hours at a time,)

sur mes yeux, fermant mes paupières,
over my eyes, closing my eyelids,

de cette odeur je m'enivrais
with that fragrance I became drunk

et dans la nuit je te voyais!
and in the night I used to see you!

Je me prenais à te <u>m</u>audire,
I began to curse you,

à te <u>d</u>étester, à me dire:
to detest you, to say to myself:

pourquoi faut-il que le destin
why is it necessary that destiny

l'ait mise là sur mon chemin?
put her there, across my path?

Puis je m'accusais de blasphème,
Then I accused myself of blasphemy,

et je ne sentais en moi-même,
and I did not feel in myself,

qu'un seul désir, un seul espoir:
but one desire, one only hope:

te revoir, ô Carmen, oui, te revoir!
you see again, oh Carmen, yes, see you again!

Car tu n'avais eu qu'à paraître,
For you wouldn't have had but to appear,

qu'à jeter un regard sur moi,
but to throw a glance towards me,

pour t'emparer de tout mon être, ô ma Carmen!
to take possession of all my being, oh my Carmen!

Et j'étais une chose à toi!
And I meant something to you!
(And that I meant something to you!)

Carmen, je t'aime!
Carmen, I love you!

CARMEN
Non, tu ne m'aimes pas!
No, you don't love me!

JOSÉ
Que dis-tu?
What say you?

CARMEN
Non, tu ne m'aimes pas, non!

Car si tu m'aimais, là-bas tu me suivrais.
For if you loved me, over there you would follow me.

JOSÉ
Carmen!

CARMEN
Oui! . . . là-bas dans la montagne,
Yes! . . . down there into the mountain(s),

là-bas tu me suivrais,

sur ton cheval tu me prendrais,
on your horse you would take me,

et comme un brave à travers la campagne,
and like a daredevil across the countryside,

en croupe tu m'emporterais!
on your horse's rump you would take me!

JOSÉ
Carmen!

CARMEN
Là-bas tu me suivrais, si tu m'aimais!

Tu n'y dépendrais de personne;
You wouldn't depend on anyone;

point d'officier à qui tu doives obéir
no officer to whom you must obey

et point de retraite qui sonne
and not some retreat that sounds

pour dire à l'amoureux qu'il est temps de partir!
to tell the lover that it is time to leave!

Le ciel ouvert, la vie errante,
The sky open, the life wandering,

pour pays tout l'univers; et pour loi sa volonté,
for country the entire universe; and for law, your own will,

et surtout la chose enivrante: la liberté!
and above all the thing intoxicating: Freedom!

JOSÉ
Mon Dieu!
My God!

CARMEN
Là-bas dans la montagne, etc.

JOSÉ
Ah! Carmen, hélas! Tais-toi! Pitié!
Ah, Carmen, alas! Be quiet! (Have) pity!

CARMEN
Oui, n'est-ce pas, là-bas tu me suivras,
Yes, it isn't it so, down there you will follow me,

Là-bas emporte-moi!
Down there take me!

JOSÉ
Ah! Tais-toi!
Ah, be quiet!

Ah! Je ne veux plus t'écouter!
Ah! I don't want any longer to listen to you!

Quitter mon drapeau . . . déserter . . .
Abandon my flag . . . to desert . . .

C'est la honte, c'est l'infamie! Je n'en veux pas!
It's the shame, it's cowardice! I want no part of it!

CARMEN
Eh bien, pars!
All right, leave!

JOSÉ
Carmen, je t'en prie!
Carmen, I beg you!

CARMEN
Non! Je ne t'aime plus!
No! I don't love you anymore!

JOSÉ
Écoute!
Listen!

CARMEN
Va! Je te hais! Adieu! Mais adieu pour jamais!
Go! I hate you! Good-bye! But good-bye forever!

JOSÉ
Eh bien, soit . . . adieu pour jamais!
All right, so be it . . . good-bye forever!

CARMEN
Va-t'en!
Get out!

JOSÉ
Carmen! adieu! adieu pour jamais!

(Don José va en courant jusqu'à la porte; au moment où il y arrive, on frappe.)
(José runs towards the door and a knock is heard. José and Carmen stop to listen. Another knock.)

NO. 18 FINALE
NO. 18 FINALE

ZUNIGA
(au dehors)
(from outside the door)
Holà Carmen! Holà!
Hello there, Carmen! Hello!

JOSÉ
Qui frappe? Qui vient là?
Who is knocking? Who is coming?

CARMEN
Tais-toi!
Be quiet!

ZUNIGA
(faisant sauter la porte)
(brusquely opening the door and coming in)
J'ouvre moi-même et j'entre.
I open myself and I enter.

(il voit Don José)
(He sees Don José.)

Ah! Fi! La belle! Le choix n'est pas heureux!
Ah, fie, my pretty! The choice is not happy!

C'est se mésallier de prendre le soldat
It's an unsuitable alliance to take a soldier

quand on a l'officier.
when one has an officer.

(à Don José)
(to José)

Allons! Décampe!
Let's go! Off with you!

JOSÉ
Non!
No!

ZUNIGA
Si fait, tu partiras!
Most certainly, you will leave!

JOSÉ
Je ne partirai pas!
I won't leave!

ZUNIGA
(le frappant)
(slapping him)
Drôle!
Fool!

JOSÉ
(sautant sur son sabre)
(getting his saber)
Tonnerre! Il va pleuvoir des coups!
By thunder! It's going to rain some blows!
(By thunder, I am going to rain blows on you!)
(I am going to beat you up!)

CARMEN
(se jetant entre eux deux)
(jumping between them)
Au diable le jaloux!
To the devil, the jealous one!

(appellant)
(calling out)

À moi!
Help!

(Les bohémiens paraissent de tous les côtés. Carmen d'un geste montre Zuniga aux bohémiens. Le Dancaïre et Le Remendado se jettent sur lui, le désarment.)
(The gypsies appear from all sides; Dancairo and Remendado go to Zuniga and disarm him. The gypsies keep a firm hold on him.)

CARMEN
(taquin à Zuniga)
(teasingly, to Zuniga)
Bel officier! L'amour vous joue
My handsome officer! Love plays on you

en ce moment un assez vilain tour.
at this moment a rather dirty trick.

Vous arrivez fort mal, hélas!
You arrive at a bad time, alas!

Et nous sommes forcés, ne voulant être dénoncés,
And we are forced, not wanting to be denounced (to the police),

de vous garder au moins . . . pendant une heure.
to keep you at least . . . for an hour.

LE DANCAÏRE et LE REMENDADO
DANCAIRO, REMENDADO
(moqueur)
(mockingly)
Mon cher monsieur, nous allons, s'il vous plaît, quitter cette demeure;
My dear sir, we will go, if you please, leave this dwelling;

vous viendrez avec nous?
you will come with us?

CARMEN
C'est une promenade.
It's a stroll.

LE DANCAÏRE et LE REMENDADO
DANCAIRO, REMENDADO
(tenant un pistolet à la tête)
(putting a pistol to his head)
Consentez-vous? Répondez, camarade.
Do you consent? Answer, comrade.

TOUS LES BOHÉMIENS
ALL GYPSIES
Répondez, camarade.
Answer, comrade.

ZUNIGA
Certainement, d'autant plus que votre argument
Certainly, the more so since your argument

est un de ceux auxquels on ne résiste guère.
is one of those to which one cannot resist hardly.
(is one that can hardly be resisted.)

mais gare à vous! Plus tard!
but watch out for yourselves! Later!

LE DANCAÏRE
DANCAIRO
La guerre, c'est la guerre! En attendant, mon officier,
War, it's war! Meanwhile, my officer,

passez devant sans vous faire prier.
go ahead without having to be asked (again).

LE REMENDADO et LES BOHÉMIENS
REMENDADO and GYPSIES
Passez devant sans vous faire prier!

(L'officier sort, emmené par quatre bohémiens, le pistolet à la main.)
(Zuniga is taken away, followed by several gypsies with their pistols trained on him.)

CARMEN
(à Don José)
(to José)
Es-tu des nôtres maintenant?
Are you one of ours now?
(Are you now one of us?)

Agnes Baltsa as Carmen and José Carreras as Don José, 1987
ERIKA DAVIDSON / METROPOLITAN OPERA ARCHIVES

Waltraud Meier as Carmen and Plácido Domingo as Don José, 1996

René Pape as Escamillo, 2000
Erika Davidson / Metropolitan Opera Archives

Olga Borodina as Carmen and Ildar Abdrazakov
as Escamillo, 2004
KEN HOWARD / METROPOLITAN OPERA

Denyce Graves as Carmen, 2005
KEN HOWARD / METROPOLITAN OPERA

Elina Garanča as Carmen, 2009
Ken Howard / Metropolitan Opera

Jonas Kaufmann as Don José, 2010

Anita Rachvelishvili as Carmen, 2012
KEN HOWARD / METROPOLITAN OPERA

JOSÉ
Il le faut bien.
I have to, indeed.
(I have no alternative.)

CARMEN
Ah! Le mot n'est pas galant,
Ah! That word is not gallant,
(That was not so gallantly put,)

mais qu'importe, va, tu t'y feras quand tu verras
but no matter, go, you will take to it there when you see

comme c'est beau la vie errante,
how it is beautiful the life wandering,
(how beautiful a wandering life can be)

pour pays l'univers, et pour loi sa volonté,
for (a) country the universe, and for law your own will,

et surtout, la chose enivrante: la liberté!
and above all, the thing entoxicating: Freedom!

TOUS
ALL
(à Don José)
(to José)
Suis-nous à travers la campagne,
Follow us across the countryside,

viens avec nous dans la montagne,
come with us to the mountain,

suis-nous et tu t'y feras, quand tu verras là-bas,
follow us and you'll take to it, when you see there,

**comme c'est beau la vie errante; pour pays l'univers, et pour loi,
sa volonté!, etc.**

Le ciel ouvert!
The sky open!
(The open sky!)

La vie errante, et surtout la chose enivrante, la liberté!

*(Au milieu de l'agitation générale, José et Carmen embrasser; autant
de cris se fait entendre dans les gitans.)*
*(In the midst of general commotion, José and Carmen embrace; much shout-
ing is heard from the gypsies.)*

FIN DE L'ACTE II
END OF ACT II

TROISIÈME ACTE
ACT III

(Site pittoresque et sauvage—solitude complète et nuit noire. Prélude musical. Un contrebandier paraît au haut des rochers, puis un autre, puis deux autres, puis vingt autres çà et là, descendant et escaladant les rochers. Des hommes portent de gros ballots sur les épaules.)
(It is a very dark night on a wild mountain pass, with large rocks everywhere. A smuggler, lantern in hand, appears above a rock, signaling his companions in the distance. Soon he is joined by others, some of them carrying heavy bales on their shoulders.)

CHŒUR
CHORUS
Écoute, compagnon, écoute, la fortune est là-bas,
Listen, friend, listen, the fortune lies over there,

mais prends garde pendant la route de faire un faux pas!
but take care along the way to take a wrong step!
(but watch your step along the way!)

SEXTET

**JOSÉ, CARMEN, FRASQUITA, MERCÉDÈS, LE DANCAÏRE, et
LE REMENDADO**
**JOSÉ, CARMEN, FRASQUITA, MERCÉDÈS, DANCAIRO, and
REMENDADO**
Notre métier est bon,
Our occupation is good,

mais pour le faire il faut avoir une âme forte!
but to carry it out you must have a soul hardy!

Et le péril est en haut,[1] il est en bas,
And (the) danger is above, it is below,

il est partout, qu'importe!
it is everywhere, no matter!

Nous allons devant nous sans souci du torrent,
We go forward without worrying about the torrent,

sans souci de l'orage,
without worrying about the storm,

sans souci du soldat qui là-bas nous attend,
without worrying about the soldier who there us awaits,
(without worrying about the soldier who waits for us down there,)

et nous guette au passage . . . sans souci nous allons en avant.
and keeps a sharp watch for (our) passage . . . without care we go
onward.

TOUS
ALL
Écoute, compagnon, écoute, etc.

NO. 19 BIS RÉCITATIVE
NO. 19 BIS RECITATIVE

LE DANCAÏRE
DANCAIRO
Reposons-nous une heure ici, mes camarades;
Let us rest one hour here, my comrades;

nous, nous allons nous rassurer que le chemin² est libre,
we, we will go satisfy ourselves that the path is clear,

et que sans algarades la contrebande peut passer.
and that unmolested, the contraband can get through.

(Pendant la scène entrent Carmen et José. Quelques bohémiens allument un feu près duquel Mercédès et Frasquita viennent s'asseoir. Les autres se roulent dans leurs manteaux, se couchent et s'endorment.)
(Carmen and José enter. Some of the gypsies light a fire. Frasquita and Mercédès sit by it and take out decks of cards. The others wrap themselves in their cloaks and try to sleep.)

CARMEN
(à José)
(to José)
Que regardes-tu donc?
What are you looking at then?

JOSÉ
Je me dis que là-bas
I am telling myself that down there

il existe une bonne et vieille femme
there lives a good and aged woman

qui me croit[3] honnête homme.
who believes me to be (an) honest man.

Elle se trompe, hélas!
She is mistaken, alas!

CARMEN
Qui donc est cette femme?
Who then is this woman?

JOSÉ
Ah! Carmen, sur mon âme, ne raille pas . . . car c'est ma mère.
Ah! Carmen, by my soul, don't rail against me . . . for it's my mother.

CARMEN
Eh bien! Va la retrouver tout de suite!
Ah well! Go find her right away!

Notre métier, vois-tu, ne te vaut rien.
Our business, you see, doesn't mean to you anything.

Et tu ferais fort bien de partir au plus vite.
And you would do very well to leave as soon as possible.

JOSÉ
Partir, nous séparer?
Leave, separate from each other?

CARMEN
Sans doute.
Without doubt.

JOSÉ
Nous séparer, Carmen? Écoute, si tu redis ce mot!
Leave you, Carmen? Listen, if you say again that word!

CARMEN
Tu me tuerais peut-être?
You would kill me, perhaps?

Quel regard, tu ne réponds rien . . .
What a look, you don't answer anything . . .

Que m'importe, après tout, le destin est le maître.
What do I care, after all, (the) destiny is our master.

NO. 19 TRIO

FRASQUITA et MERCÉDÈS
FRASQUITA and MERCÉDÈS
(avec jeu de cartes)
(with decks of cards)
Mêlons! Coupons! Bien, c'est cela!
Shuffle! Cut! Good, that's that!

Trois cartes ici, quattre là!
Three cards here, four there!

Et maintenant, parlez, mes belles,
And now, speak, my pretties,

de l'avenir, donnez-nous des nouvelles;
of the future, give us some news;

dites-nous qui nous trahira,
tell us who will betray us,

dites-nous qui nous aimera! Parlez!
tell us who will love us! Speak!

FRASQUITA
Moi, je vois un jeune amoureux,
Me, I see a young suitor,

qui m'aime on ne peut davantage.
who loves me one cannot more.

MERCÉDÈS
Le mien est très riche et très vieux,
(The) mine is very rich and very old,

mais il parle de mariage.
but he speaks of marriage.

FRASQUITA
Je me campe sur son cheval,
I settle myself on his horse,

et dans la montagne il m'entraîne.
and to the mountain he carries me off.

MERCÉDÈS
Dans un château presque royal,
In a castle almost royal,

le mien m'installe en souveraine!
(the) mine sets me up like a queen!

FRASQUITA
De l'amour à n'en plus finir,
Love making to never end,

tous les jours nouvelles follies!
all the days new raptures!

MERCÉDÈS
De l'or tant que j'en puis tenir,
Gold as much as I can hold,

des diamants, des pierreries!
diamonds (and) precious stones!

FRASQUITA
Le mien devient un chef fameux,[4]
Mine becomes a leader famous,

cent hommes marchent à sa suite!
a hundred men march in his retinue!

MERCÉDÈS
Le mien, en croirai-je mes yeux?
Mine, can I believe my eyes?

Oui, il meurt! Ah! Ce suis veuve et j'hérite!
Yes, he dies! Ah! I am widow and I inherit

Parlez encor, parlez mes belles, etc.

MERCÉDÈS
Fortune!
Fortune!

FRASQUITA
Amour!
Love!

(Ils remontent à la consultation de leurs cartes.)
(They go back to consulting their cards.)

CARMEN
(en prenant certaines cartes)
(taking some cards)
Voyons, que j'essaie à mon tour.
Let's see, let me try at my turn.
(let me have a turn.)

(Elle se met à tourner les cartes.)
(She starts turning the cards over.)

Carreau, pique . . . la mort!
Diamonds, spades . . . death!

J'ai bien lu . . . moi d'abord,
I have clearly read . . . I first,

ensuite lui . . . pour tous les deux la mort!
then he . . . for the two of us death!

(Elle continue de brouiller les cartes.)
(She continues to shuffle the cards.)

En vain pour éviter les réponses amères,
In vain to avoid the replies bitter,

en vain tu mêleras;
in vain you will shuffle;

cela ne sert[5] à rien, les cartes sont sincères et ne mentiront pas!
that is of no avail, (for) the cards are sincere and will not lie!

Dans le livre d'en haut si ta page est heureuse,
In the book above if your page is happy,
(If your page in the heavenly book is a happy one,)

mêle et coupe sans peur,
shuffle and cut without fear,

la carte sous tes doigts se tournera joyeuse,
the card under your fingers will turn up happy,

t'annonçant le bonheur.
fortelling you good luck.

Mais si tu dois mourir,
But if you must die,

si le mot redoubtable est écrit par le sort,
if the word terrible is written by the fate,

recommence vingt fois, la carte impitoyable répétera: la mort!
begin over twenty times, the card pitiless will repeat: death!

(tournant les cartes)
(She turns the cards over again and again.)

Encor! Encor! Toujours la mort!
Again! Again! Always death!

FRASQUITA et MERCÉDÈS
Parlez encor, parlez mes belles, etc.

CARMEN
Encore! Le désespoir! Toujours la mort!
Again! The despair! Always death!

(Le Dancaïre et Le Remendado rentrent.)
(Dancairo and Remendado re-enter.)

NO. 20 BIS RÉCITATIVE
NO. 20 BIS RECITATIVE

CARMEN
Eh bien?
Well?

LE DANCAÏRE
DANCAIRO
Eh bien! Nous essayerons de passer et nous passerons;
Well! We will try to get through and we will get through;

reste là-haut, José, garde les marchandises.
stay up there, José, guard the merchandise.

FRASQUITA
La route, est-elle libre?
The way, is it open?

LE DANCAÏRE
DANCAIRO
Oui, mais gare aux surprises!
Yes, but watch out for surprises!

J'ai sur la brèche où nous devons passer vu trois douaniers;
I have on the pass, where we must pass, seen three customs agents;

il faut nous en débarrasser.
it is necessary that we get rid of them.

CARMEN
Prenez les ballots⁶ et partons;
Take the bales and let us go;

il faut passer, nous passerons!
we must pass, we will pass!

NO. 21 ENSEMBLE AVEC CHORUS
NO. 21 ENSEMBLE WITH CHORUS

CARMEN, FRASQUITA, MERCÉDÈS
Quant au douanier, c'est notre affaire,
As far as (the) customs man, it's our business,

tout comme un autre il aime à plaire,
just like any other man he loves to please,

il aime à faire le galant!
he loves to play the gallant swain!

Ah! Laissez-nous passer en avant!
Ah! Let us pass ahead!

TOUTES LES FEMMES
ALL THE WOMEN
Quant au douanier, etc.

TOUS
ALL
Il aime à plaire!
He loves to please!

MERCÉDÈS
Le douanier sera clément!
The customs man will be clement!
(The customs man will go easy on us.)

TOUS
ALL
Il est galant!
He is gallant!

CARMEN
Le douanier sera charmant!
The customs man will be charming!

TOUS
ALL
Il aime à plaire!

FRASQUITA
Le douanier sera galant!

MERCÉDÈS
Oui, le douanier sera même entreprenant!
Yes, the customs man will be even forward!
(Yes, the customs man may even make a pass at us!)

TOUS
ALL
Oui, le douanier c'est notre affaire, etc.

CARMEN, FRASQUITA, MERCÉDÈS
Il ne s'agit plus de bataille,
It's no longer a question of battle,

non, il s'agit tout simplement
no, it's a question quite simply

de se laisser prendre la taille
of allowing ourselves (to be) taken (by) the waist

et d'écouter un compliment.
and to listen to a compliment.

S'il faut aller jusqu'au sourire,
If we need to go as far as a smile,

que voulez-vous, on sourira!
what do you want, we will smile!

TOUTES LES FEMMES
ALL WOMEN
Et d'avance je puis le dire,
And here and now I can say it,

la contrebande passera!
the contraband will go through!

En avant! Marchons! Allons!
Forward! Let's walk! Let's go!

(Tout le monde sort. José ferme la marche et sort en examinant l'amorce de sa carabine; un peu avant qu'il soit sorti, on voit un homme passer sa tête au-dessus du rocher. C'est le guide de Micaëla.)
(The gypsies begin to leave. José brings up the rear. As soon as all are out of sight, Micaëla appears, led by a guide. She gives him some money and the guide leaves.)

NO. 22 ARIA

MICAËLA
C'est des contrebandiers le refuge ordinaire.
It is of the smugglers the refuge usual.
(This is the usual haunt of the smugglers.)

Il est ici, je le verrai . . .
He is here, I will see him . . .

et le devoir que m'imposa sa mère
and the duty that on me laid his mother

sans trembler je l'accomplirai.
without trembling I will carry out.

Je dis que rien ne m'épouvante,
I say that nothing cannot frighten me,

je dis, hélas, que je réponds de moi;
I say, alas, that I answer for myself;
(I say, alas, that I have only myself to depend on;)

mais j'ai beau faire la vaillante,
but I tried in vain to play the valiant one,

au fond du cœur je meurs d'effroi!
in the bottom of (my) heart I die of fear!

Seule, en ce lieu sauvage,
Alone, in this place wild,

toute seule j'ai peur, mais j'ai tort d'avoir peur;
all alone I am afraid, but I do wrong to have fear;

vous me protégerez, Seigneur.
thou will protect me, Lord.

Je vais voir de près cette femme
I will look from close by that woman
(I am going to get a close look at that woman)

dont les artifices <u>m</u>audits
whose wiles cursed

ont fini par faire un infâme
did finish by making a criminal

de celui que j'aimais jadis.
of him whom I loved once.
(whose cursed wiles have finished by making a criminal of the man
I once loved.)

Elle est dangereuse, elle est belle,
She is dangerous, she is beautiful,

mais je ne veux pas avoir peur,
but I don't want to have fear,
(but I don't want to be afraid,)

je parlerai haut devant elle, ah!
I will speak loud before her, ah!
(I will speak out to her!)

Seigneur, vous me protégerez!
Lord, you will protect me!

NO. 22 BIS RÉCITATIVE
NO. 22 BIS RECITATIVE

MICAËLA
(voir José-dessus)
(seeing José up above)
Je ne me trompe pas . . . c'est lui sur ce rocher. À moi, José!
I am not mistaken . . . it's he on that rock. This way, José!

Je ne puis approcher.
I cannot come nearer.

Mais que fait-il? Il ajuste, il fait feu.
But what is he doing? He is aiming, he is firing.

(On entend un coup de feu.)
(The report of a rifle shot is heard.)

Ah! J'ai trop présumé de mes forces, mon Dieu.
Ah! I did too much presume of my strength, my God!
(Ah my God, I overestimated my strength!)

(Elle disparaît derrière les rochers. Au meme moment entre Escamillo tenant son chapeau à la main.)
(She disappears behind the rock while at the same time Escamillo enters, hat in hand.)

NO. 23 SCÈNE ET DUO
NO. 23 SCENE AND DUET

ESCAMILLO
(regardant son chapeau)
(looking at his hat which has just been shot off his head)
Quelques lignes plus bas et tout[7] était fini.
A few inches lower and all would be over.

JOSÉ
(son couteau à la main)
(knife in hand)
Votre nom, répondez!
Your name, answer!

ESCAMILLO
Eh! Doucement, l'ami!
Hey! Easy does it, my friend!

Je suis[8] Escamillo, toréro de Grenade!
I am Escamillo, bullfighter from Granada!

JOSÉ
Escamillo!

ESCAMILLO
C'est moi!
It is I!

JOSÉ
(remettant son couteau à sa ceinture)
(returning his knife to its sheath)
Je connais votre nom,
I know your name,

soyez le bienvenu, mais vraiment, camarade,
be welcome, but truly (my) comrade,

vous pouviez y rester.[9]
you could have died.
(I could have shot you dead.)

ESCAMILLO
Je ne vous dis pas non,
I won't say no,
(I won't deny that)

mais je suis amoureux, mon cher, à la folie,
but I am in love, my friend, to madness,
(I am madly in love, my friend,)

et celui-là serait un pauvre compagnon,
and he would be a wretched fellow,

qui, pour voir ses amours, ne risquerait sa vie.
who, to see his lady love, wouldn't risk his life.

JOSÉ
Celle que vous aimez est ici?
She whom you love is here?

ESCAMILLO
Justement. C'est une zingara, mon cher.
Exactly. She's a gypsy, my friend.

JOSÉ
Elle s'appelle?
She is called?
(What is her name?)

ESCAMILLO
Carmen.

JOSÉ
Carmen!

ESCAMILLO
Carmen, oui, mon cher. Elle avait pour amant
Carmen, yes, my friend. She used to have for a lover

un soldat qui jadis a déserté pour elle.
a soldier who once did desert for her sake.

Ils s'adoraient, mais c'est fini, je crois.
They adored one another, but it's over, I think.

Les amours de Carmen ne durent pas six mois.
The loves of Carmen don't last past six months.

JOSÉ
Vous l'aimez cependant?
You love her still?
(And despite the fact that her loves do not last past six months you still love her?)

ESCAMILLO
Je l'aime! Oui, mon cher, je l'aime à la folie.
I love her, yes, my friend, I love her madly.

JOSÉ
Mais pour nous enlever nos filles de bohème,
But to take from us our gypsy girls,

savez-vous bien qu'il faut payer?
do you know that you have to pay?

ESCAMILLO
Soit! on paiera.
So be it! I will pay.

JOSÉ
Et que le prix se paie à coups de *navaja*.
And that the price is paid with blows from a *navaja*.[10]

ESCAMILLO
À coups de *navaja*!
With a *navaja*!

JOSÉ
Le discours est très net.
The speech is very clear.

ESCAMILLO
Ce déserteur, ce beau soldat qu'elle aime,
That deserter, that handsome soldier whome she loves,

ou du moins qu'elle aimait . . . c'est donc vous?
or at least she *loved* . . . is then you?

JOSÉ
Oui, c'est moi-même!
Yes, it's me myself!

ESCAMILLO
J'en suis ravi, mon cher, et le tour est complet!
I am delighted, my friend, and the turn is completed!
(and the wheel's come full circle!)

*(**Tous les deux tirent la navaja** et s'entourent le bras gauche de leurs manteaux.)*
(Both draw their navajas and wrap their free arms in their cloaks, crouching low and assuming fighting positions.)

JOSÉ
Enfin ma colère trouve à qui parler!
At last my anger finds someone (to) whom to speak!
(At last my rage has found an outlet!)

Le sang, je l'espère, va bientôt couler.
The blood, I hope, will soon flow.

ESCAMILLO
Quelle maladresse, j'en rirai vraiment!
What awkwardness, I will laugh about it, really!

Chercher la maîtresse et trouver l'amant!
To look for the mistress and find her lover!

ESCAMILLO, JOSÉ
Mettez-vous en garde, et veillez sur vous!
Put up your guard, and look out for yourself!

Tant pis pour qui tarde à parer les coups!
So much the worse for who delays in parrying the thrusts!

En garde! Allons! Veillez sur vous!
On guard! Let's go! Look out for yourself!

(Combat. Le Toréro glisse et tombe. Entrent Carmen et Le Dancaïre. Carmen arrête le bras de Don José. Le Toréro se relève; Le Remendado, Mercédès, Frasquita et les contrebandiers rentrent pendant ce temps.)
(They fight. The torero elegantly avoids José's thrusts as if he were sidestepping a furious charging bull. He then slips and falls. José is about to stab him when Carmen and the others arrive on the scene. José is disarmed and held by the gypsies.)

NO. 24 FINALE
NO. 24 FINAL

CARMEN
(se précipiter pour José)
(rushing to José)
Holà! José!
Stop, José!

ESCAMILLO
Vrai, j'ai l'âme ravie
Truly, I have my soul overjoyed

que ce soit vous, Carmen, qui me sauviez la vie!
that it be you, Carmen, who saved me the life!
(Truly I am overjoyed that it was you, Carmen, who saved my life!)

(à Don José)
(to José)

Quant à toi, beau soldat,
As for you, handsome soldier,

nous sommes manche à manche,
we are even,
(we've reached a stalemate,)

et nous jouerons la belle le jour où tu voudras
and we will gamble for the pretty one the day that you want

reprendre le combat!
to renew the fight!

LE DANCAÏRE
DANCAIRO
C'est bon, plus de querelles, nous allons partir.
All right, no more quarreling, we are going to leave.

(au Toréro)
(to Escamillo)

Et toi, l'ami, bonsoir!
And you, my friend, good night!

ESCAMILLO
Souffrez au moins qu'avant de vous dire au revoir,
Permit at least that before I say to you good-bye,

je vous invite tous aux courses de Séville.
I you invite all of you to the *corrida*[11] in Seville.

Je compte pour ma part y briller de mon mieux,
I can count on my part there to shine at my best,

et qui m'aime y viendra.
and whoever loves me, there will come.

(à Don José qui fait un geste de menace)
(to José, who makes a threatening gesture)

L'ami, tiens-toi tranquille,
My friend, keep yourself calm,

j'ai tout dit, oui, j'ai tout dit,
I have all said, yes, I've said it all,

et je n'ai plus ici qu'à faire mes adieux.
And I haven't any longer here but to bid my good-byes.
(and I have nothing else to do but to say good-bye.)

(Jeu de scène. Don José veut s'élancer sur le Toréro. Le Dancaïre et Le Remendado le retiennent. Le Toréro sort très lentement.)
(José tries to rush Escamillo but is restrained by the gypsies. Escamillo leaves slowly, looking back at Carmen, who watches him in some fascination.)

JOSÉ
(à Carmen)
(to Carmen)
Prends garde à toi, Carmen, je suis las de souffrir!
Watch out for yourself, Carmen, I am tired of suffering!

(Carmen lui répond par un léger haussement d'épaules et s'éloigne de lui.)
(Carmen's reply is a shrugging of her shoulders. She walks away.)

LE DANCAÏRE
DANCAIRO
En route, il faut partir!
On our way! We must leave!

TOUS
ALL
En route, il faut partir!

LE REMENDADO
REMENDADO
Halte! Quelqu'un[12] est là qui cherche à se cacher!
Stop! Someone is there who is trying to hide himself!

(Il amène Micaëla.)
(He goes over and brings out the frightened Micaëla.)

CARMEN
Une femme!
A woman!

LE DANCAÏRE
DANCAIRO
Pardieu! La surprise est heureuse!
By God! The surprise is pleasant!

JOSÉ
Micaëla!

MICAËLA
Don José!

JOSÉ
Malheureuse! Que viens-tu faire ici?
Poor girl! What come you to do here?

MICAËLA
Moi, je viens te chercher.
Me, I come looking for you.

Là-bas est la chaumière,
Down there is the cottage,

où sans cesse priant
where without stopping, praying

une mère, ta mère, pleure, hélas, sur son enfant.
a mother, your mother, weeps, alas, over her son.

Elle pleure et t'appelle,
She weeps and calls you,

elle pleure et te tend les bras;
she weeps and holds out to you her arms;

tu prendras pitié d'elle,
you will take pity on her,

José, ah! José, tu me suivras!
José, ah! José, you will follow me!

CARMEN
(avec dédain)
(disdainfully)
Va-t'en! Tu feras bien,
Go on! You will do well,

notre métier ne te vaut rien!
our business means nothing to you!

JOSÉ
Tu me dis de la suivre?
You are telling me to follow her?

CARMEN
Oui, tu devrais partir!
Yes, you should leave!

JOSÉ
Tu me dis de la suivre?

Pour que toi, tu puisses courir après ton nouvel amant!
So that you, you can run after your new lover!

Non! Non vraiment! Dût-il m'en coûter la vie,
No! Not likely! Should it even cost me my life,

non, Carmen, je ne partirai pas,
no, Carmen, I will not leave,

et la chaîne qui nous lie, nous liera jusqu'au trépas!
and the chain that us bind, will bind us until death!

Dût-il m'en coûter la vie, non, je ne partirai pas! etc.

MICAËLA
Écoute-moi, je t'en prie, ta mère te tend les bras,
Listen to me, I beg you, your mother holds out to you her arms,

cette chaîne qui te lie, José, tu la briseras!
the chain that binds you, José, you will break it!

**FRASQUITA, MERCÉDÈS, LE REMENDADO, LE DANCAÏRE
et CHŒUR**
**FRASQUITA, MERCÉDÈS, REMENDADO, DANCAIRO, and
CHORUS**
Il t'en coûtera la vie, José, si tu ne pars pas,
It will cost you your life, José, if you don't leave,

et la chaîne qui vous lie se rompra par ton trépas.
and the chain that binds you will break by your death.

JOSÉ
(à Micaëla)
(to Micaëla)
Laisse-moi! Car je suis condamné!
Leave me! For I am doomed!

MICAËLA
Hélas, José!
Alas, José!

**FRASQUITA, MERCÉDÈS, LE REMENDADO, LE DANCAÏRE
et CHŒUR**
**FRASQUITA, MERCÉDÈS, REMENDADO, DANCAIRO, and
CHORUS**
José, prends garde!
José, be careful!

JOSÉ
(Carmen saisir par les cheveux pour la forcer vers le bas)
(seizing Carmen by the hair and forcing her down)

Ah! Je te tiens, fille damnée,
Ah! I have got you, girl damned,

et je te forcerai bien
and I will force you indeed

à subir la destinée qui rive ton sort au mien!
to bow to the destiny that links your fate to mine!

Dût-il m'en coûter la vie, non non je ne partirai pas!

CHŒUR
CHORUS
Prends garde! Don José!
Be careful, Don José!

MICAËLA
(autorité, à José)
(authoritatively, to José)
Une parole encor, ce sera la dernière.
One word more, it will be my last.

Hélas, José, ta mère se meurt, et ta mère
Alas, José, your mother is dying, and your mother

ne voudrait pas mourir sans t'avoir pardonné.
wouldn't want to die without having forgiven you.

JOSÉ
Ma mère! Elle se meurt!
My mother! She is dying!

MICAËLA
Oui, Don José.
Yes, Don José.

JOSÉ
Ah! Partons!
Ah, let us go!

(Carmen, dans la plus grande rage)
(to Carmen, in utmost rage)

Sois contente, je pars,
Be happy, I am leaving,

mais nous nous reverrons!
but we will meet again!

(Il s'en va, en tenant Micaëla avec lui. De loin le toréro est entendue chanter. Carmen écoute.)
(He goes off, taking Micaëla with him. From afar the bullfighter is heard singing. Carmen listens.)

ESCAMILLO
Toréador, en garde, etc.

FIN DE L'ACTE III
END OF ACT III

QUATRIÈME ACTE
ACT IV

(Une place à Séville, au fond du théâtre les murailles de la vieille arène. L'entrée du cirque est fermée par un long vélum. C'est le jour d'un combat de taureaux. Grand mouvement sur la place. Marchands d'eau, d'oranges, d'éventails, etc.)

(A square in Seville, with the exterior walls of the bullring in the background. There is great excitement, as a bullfight is about to take place, with Escamillo as its headliner. Vendors move amid the crowd, hawking water, oranges, fans, etc.)

CHŒUR
CHORUS
À deux quartos!¹ Des éventails pour s'éventer!
At two quarters! Some fans to fan yourselves!

Des oranges pour grignoter!
Some oranges to nibble!

Le programme avec les détails! De l'eau!
The program with the details! Some water!

Du vin! Des cigarettes! Voyez! À deux cuartos! *Señoras* **et caballeros!**
Some wine! Cigarettes! Look! At two quarters! Ladies and gentlemen!

ZUNIGA
Des oranges, vite!
Some oranges, quickly!

PLUSIEURS MARCHANDS
SEVERAL FRUIT SELLERS
(*se précipitant*)
(*crowding around*)
En voici, prenez, mesdemoiselles.
Here they are, take, young ladies.

UN MARCHAND
ONE FRUIT SELLER
Merci, mon officier, merci.
Thank you, my officer, thank you.

LES AUTRES MARCHANDS
THE OTHER VENDORS
Celles-ci, Señor, sont plus belles!
These here, *señor*, are prettier!

ZUNIGA
Holà! Des éventails!
Ho there! The fans!
(Hey! Fan lady!)

UNE BOHÉMIENNE
A GYPSY
(*se précipitant*)
(*running to him*)
Voulez-vous aussi des lorgnettes?
Would you want also some opera glasses?

(On entend de grand cris au dehors, des fanfares; c'est l'arrivée de la quadrille.)
(A loud roar is heard from offstage, followed by fanfares; it is the arrival of Escamillo's quadrilla.[2])

NO. 26 MARCHE ET CHŒUR
NO. 26 MARCH AND CHORUS

CHŒUR
CHORUS
Les voici! Voici la quadrille! La quadrille des toréros!
Here they are! Here's the *cuadrilla*! The *cuadrilla* of the bullfighters!

Sur les lances le soleil brille!
On the lances the sun flashes!

En l'air toques et sombreros!
In the air caps and hats![3]

Voici, débouchant sur la place,
There, emerging on the square,

voici d'abord, marchant au pas,
there, first, walking in step,

L'alguazil à vilaine face! À bas!
the *alguacil*[4] has (an) ugly mug! Down with him!

Et puis saluons au passage,
And then let us cheer as they go past,

saluons les hardis chulos!
Let us cheer the brave *chulos*![5]

Bravo! Viva! Gloire au courage!
Bravo! Hurrah! Glory to courage!

Voici les hardis chulos!

Voyez les banderilleros! Voyez quel air de crânerie!
Look at the *banderilleros!*[6] See what air of swagger!

Quel regards, et de quel éclat étincelle la broderie
What looks, and with what brilliance shines the embroidery

de leur costume de combat!
of their costume of fighting!
(of their bullfighting dress!)[7]

(Un autre* cuadrilla *apparaît.)
(Another cuadrilla *appears.)*

Une autre quadrille s'avance! Voyez les picadors!
Another *cuadrilla* is coming! Look at the picadors![8]

Comme ils sont beaux!
How they are handsome![9]

Comme ils vont du fer de leur lance,
How they go with the tips of their lances,

harceler les flancs des taureaux!
torment the flanks[10] of the bulls!

(Paraît enfin Escamillo, ayant près de lui Carmen, radieuse et dans un costume éclatant.)
(Escamillo finally appears, dressed in a handsome suit of lights. Carmen, dressed in a splendid dress, is at his side.)

L'espada! Escamillo! C'est l'espada, la fine lame,
The *espada!*[11] Escamillo! It's the *espada* of the fine blade,
(It's the *matador* with his fine sword,)

celui qui vient terminer tout!
he who comes to finish all!

Qui paraît à la fin du drame
Who appears at the end of the drama

et qui frappe le dernier coup!
and who strikes the last blow!

Vive Escamillo! Ah, bravo!, etc.

ESCAMILLO
(à Carmen)
(to Carmen)
Si tu m'aimes, Carmen,
If you love me, Carmen,

tu pourras tout à l'heure être fière de moi.
you will very soon be proud of me.

CARMEN
Oui, je t'aime, Escamillo, et que je meure
Yes, I love you, Escamillo, and may I die

si j'ai jamais aimé quelqu'un autant que toi.
If I have ever loved someone as much as you.

TOUS LES DEUX
BOTH
Ah! Je t'aime! Oui, je t'aime!

(Escamillo va dans l'arène. Carmen reste à l'extérieur.)
(Escamillo goes into the bull ring. Carmen stays outside.)

LES ALGUAZILS
THE ALGUAZILS (POLICEMEN)
Place! Place au seigneur Alcalde!
Make way! Make way for his honor (the) Mayor!

(Petite marche à l'orchestre. Sur cette marche entre au fond l'alcalde
précédé et suivi des alguazils. Pendant ce temps Frasquita et Mercédès
s'approchent de Carmen.)
(The Mayor enters, preceded by the alguazils. He is usually accompanied
by his wife. During his entrance Frasquita and Mercédès start to approach
Carmen.)

FRASQUITA
Carmen, un bon conseil, ne reste pas ici!
Carmen, some good advice, don't stay here!

CARMEN
Et pourquoi, s'il te plaît?
And why, if you please?

MERCÉDÈS
Il est là!
He is there!

CARMEN
Qui donc?
Who, then?

(José peut être vu rôder dans le fond, l'air hagard et échevelé.)
(José can be seen lurking about in the background, looking haggard and
disheveled.)

MERCÉDÈS
Lui, Don José! Dans la foule il se cache; prends garde!
He, Don José! In the crowd he is hiding; take care!

CARMEN
Oui, je le vois.
Yes, I see him.

FRASQUITA
Prends garde!

CARMEN
Je ne suis pas femme à trembler devant lui.
I am not a woman to tremble before him.

Je l'attends, et je vais lui parler.
I am expecting him, and I will to him speak.

MERCÉDÈS
Carmen, crois-moi, prends garde!
Carmen, believe me, take care!

CARMEN
Je ne crains rien!
I do not fear anything!

FRASQUITA
Prends garde!

(L'alcalde est entré dans le cirque. Derrière l'alcalde, le cortège de la quadrille reprend sa marche et entre dans le cirque. La populace suit . . . et la foule en se retirant a dégagé Don José . . . Carmen reste seule au premier plan.)

*(The Mayor and his entourage go into the bullring, followed by the populace.
José and Carmen are left alone in the square.)*

NO. 27 DUO ET FINALE CHŒUR
NO. 27 DUET AND FINAL CHORUS

CARMEN
C'est toi!
It's you!

JOSÉ
C'est moi!
It's me!

CARMEN
L'on m'avait avertie que tu n'étais pas loin,
They had told me that you weren't far,

l'on m'avait même dit de craindre pour ma vie,
they had to me even told to fear for my life,

mais je suis brave et n'ai pas voulu fuir.
but I am brave and did not wish to run away.

JOSÉ
Je ne menace pas, j'implore, je supplie;
I am not threatening, I'm imploring, I am beseeching;

notre passé, Carmen, je l'oublierai.
our past, Carmen, I will forget it.

Oui, nous allons tous deux commencer une autre vie,
Yes, we will go both of us begin another life,

loin d'ici, sous d'autres cieux!
far from here, under other skies!

CARMEN
Tu demandes l'impossible, Carmen jamais n'a menti.
You ask the impossible, Carmen has never lied.

Son âme reste inflexible.
Her soul remains inflexible.

Entre elle et toi, tout est fini.
Between she and you, all is finished.

Jamais je n'ai menti; entre nous tout est fini.
Never I have lied; between us all is over.

JOSÉ
Carmen, il est temps encore, oui, il est temps encore.
Carmen, it is time still, yes, there's time still.

Ô ma Carmen, laisse-moi te sauver, toi que j'adore,
Oh my Carmen, let me save you, you whom I adore,

et me sauver avec toi!
and save myself with you!

CARMEN
Non, je sais bien que c'est l'heure,
No, I know full well that it is the hour,

je sais bien que tu me tueras;
I know full well that you will kill me;

mais que je vive ou que je meure,
but whether I live or whether I die,

non, je ne te céderai pas!
no, I will not give in to you!

JOSÉ
Carmen, il est temps encore, etc.

CARMEN
Pourquoi t'occuper encore
Why bother yourself still

d'un cœur qui n'est plus à toi?
with a heart that is no longer yours?

En vain tu dis: "Je t'adore,"
In vain you say "I adore you,"

tu n'obtiendras rien de moi.
you won't get anything from me.

JOSÉ
(en regardant incrédule, dans le plus grand désespoir)
(looking incredulous, in utmost despair)
Tu ne m'aimes donc plus?
You don't love me anymore?

(Silence de Carmen.)
(Carmen remains silent.)

Tu ne m'aimes donc plus?

CARMEN
Non, je ne t'aime plus.
No, I don't love you anymore.

JOSÉ
Mais moi, Carmen, je t'aime encore;
But I, Carmen, I love you still;

Carmen, hélas! Moi, je t'adore!
Carmen, alas! Me, I adore you!

CARMEN
À quoi bon tout cela? Que de mots superflus!
What good is all that? What words superfluous!

JOSÉ
Carmen, je t'aime, je t'adore!

Eh bien, s'il le faut, pour te plaire,
Oh well, if it must be, to please you,

je resterai bandit, tout ce que tu voudras . . .
I will remain a bandit, all that you would want . . .

Tout, tu m'entends? Tout!
Anything, do you hear? Anything!

Mais ne me quitte pas, ô ma Carmen,
But don't leave me, oh my Carmen,

ah! Souviens-toi du passé!
ah, remember the past!

Nous nous aimions naguère!
We loved each other once!

Ah! Ne me quitte pas, Carmen!

CHŒUR et FANFARES
CHORUS and FANFARES
(dans le cirque)
(from within)
Viva! La course est belle! Viva! Sur le sable sanglant
Hurrah! The *corrida* is grand! Hurrah, over the sand bloody

le taureau s'élance! Voyez! Voyez!
the bull is charging! Look! Look!

Le taureau qu'on[12] harcèle en bondissant s'élance, voyez!
The bull that they torment, bounding is charging, look!

Frappé juste, en plein cœur, voyez! Victoire!
Struck true, right through the heart, look! Victory!

(Pendant ce chœur, silence de Carmen et de Don José . . . Tous deux écoutent . . . Don José ne perd pas Carmen de vue . . . Le chœur terminé, Carmen fait un pas vers le cirque.)
(During this chorus, Carmen and José keep silent. Upon hearing the cry "victory!" Carmen lets out an "Ah" of pride and joy. José does not lose sight of Carmen, who now hastens to the entrance of the bullring.)

JOSÉ
(se plaçant devant elle)
(barring her way)
Où vas-tu?
Where are you going?

CARMEN
Laisse-moi!
Leave me alone!

JOSÉ
Cet homme qu'on acclame, c'est ton nouvel amant!
That man they are cheering, it's your new lover!

CARMEN
Laisse-moi!
Leave me alone!

JOSÉ
Sur mon âme, tu ne passeras pas,
Upon my soul, you will not pass,

Carmen, c'est <u>moi</u> que tu suivras!
Carmen, it is I whom you will follow!

CARMEN
Laisse-moi, Don José, je ne te suivrai pas!
Let me go, Don José, I won't follow you!

JOSÉ
Tu vas le retrouver, dis tu l'aimes donc?
You are going to meet him, tell me, you love him then?

CARMEN
Je l'aime! Et devant la mort même,
I love him! And in the face of death itself,

je répéterai que je l'aime!
I will repeat that I love him!

CHŒUR
CHORUS
Viva! La course est belle, etc.

JOSÉ
Ainsi, le salut de mon âme,
So, the salvation of my soul,

je l'aurai perdu pour que toi,
I will have lost so that you,

pour que tu t'en ailles, infâme, entre ses bras, rire de moi!
so that you can go, you wretch, in his arms laugh at me!

Non, par le sang, tu n'iras pas!
No, by my blood, you will not go!

Carmen, c'est moi que tu suivras!
Carmen, it is I whom you will follow!

CARMEN
Non, jamais!
No, never!

JOSÉ
Je suis las de te menacer!
I am tired of threatening you!

CARMEN
Eh bien! Frappe-moi donc,[13] **ou laisse-moi passer!**
All right! Strike me then, or let me pass!

CHŒUR
CHORUS
Victoire!

JOSÉ
Pour la dernière fois, démon, veux-tu me suivre?
For the last time, demon, do you want to follow me?

CARMEN
Non! Cette bague autrefois tu me l'avais donnée, tiens!
No! This ring once you had to me given, there!
(No! This ring you gave me once, there!)

(Elle la jette à la volée.)
(She takes the ring off her finger and hurls it at José.)

JOSÉ
(le poignard à la main, s'avançant sur Carmen)
(taking out his dagger, advancing towards Carmen)
Eh bien, damnée!
All right, damned one!

(Carmen recule. José la poursuit. Pendant ce temps, fanfares dans le cirque. José a frappé Carmen. Elle tombe morte . . . Le vélum s'ouvre. On sort du cirque.)
(She retreats and tries to evade him. He catches her and stabs her just as the chorus inside sings the final reprise. Carmen falls dead at his feet.)

CHŒUR
CHORUS
Toréador, en garde, etc.

JOSÉ
Vous pouvez m'arrêter. C'est moi qui l'ai tuée!
You can arrest me, it is I who killed her!

Ah, Carmen, ma Carmen adorée!
Ah, Carmen, my Carmen adored!

(Escamillo paraît sur les marches du cirque. José se jette sur le corps de Carmen. Des policiers entourent José et lui détiennent.)
(Escamillo appears at the entrance of the bullring. José throws himself on Carmen's lifeless body. Some policemen surround José and hold him.)

FIN DE L'OPÉRA
END OF OPERA

NOTES

by Nico Castel

ACT I

1. This is the most commonly used version of *Carmen*, with the recitatives by Guiraud. After much experimentation with the Opéra Comique version with spoken dialogue, non-French impresarios decided that it was too long and that non-French singers simply couldn't handle that much dialogue; French impresarios themselves have decided that the dialogue interrupts the flow of the music, even when spoken by French singers. The present version is starting to have more currency again.

2. The *liaison* is "optional." One can say *D'entrer chez nous // un instant* without the *z liaison*, or one can accept a **slight** *z liaison*. The *z liaison* must be **most delicate**!

3. The word *fumée* (smoke) is pronounced as both [fy'meœ and fy'me], depending on the musical notation, which gives a note for the mute syllable in some instances but not in others.

4. This chorus was found later and inserted into the Alkor-Edition score. This score also contains the entire dialogue as well as the Guiraud recitatives. This is the time-tested G. Schirmer score.

5. The "habanera" rhythm started in Havana, Cuba (**Habana**, in Spanish), influenced by the music of the African slaves

brought over from the West African coast by the Spanish Con-
quistadores who settled the Caribbean. The term "Afro-Cuban
music" refers specifically to the music with catchy rhythms,
giving origin to today's Hispanic "salsa." The Habanera is
a slow, sensuous rhythm. The spelling is **habanera**, and not
habañera, a mistake that has been perpetuated for decades
by one of our most esteemed music publishers in their mezzo-
soprano anthology. Incidentally, a *bañera* could be construed
as a mother's terse order to a dirty child to go and jump into
the bathtub!

6. Notice the words *rebelle* and *l'appelle*. There has to be a vowel
   sound at the end of these two words, since the *l* is a voiced
   consonant.

7. This is an obvious "dig" at José, who so far hasn't paid any
   attention to her and continues to fidget with his chain.

8. The reference to *bohème* implies the gypsies' carefree, uncon-
   ventional (*bohemian*) lifestyle.

9. The French dislike the clash of identical vowels, as in *une fois
   à*. The *liaison* with a very delicate [z] is recommended.

10. Gypsies were believed to have magic powers, and when one
    was caught in some sort of magic artifice, he/she was tied up
    and made to ride a donkey through the streets while being
    flogged mercilessly.

11. Pierrre Bernac, in his useful book *The Interpretation of French
    Song*, warns us that **comical alliterations** need to be avoided
    when making *liaison*. No *liaison* is made between *prises* and *aux*,
    which would sound "comical" with the two *z*'s next to each
    other ['sœ 'sõ prizœ 'zo ʃœ'vø].

12. By "iron" she means sword, pistol, even an iron club to force
    her to confess.

13. Again, a **very slight** *liaison* with the *z*.

14. *Manzanilla* is a very dry Spanish sherry, usually served very
    cold.

15. One word about **DONC**: The word is only pronounced with a final [k] sound when it heads a sentence or phrase or when it is in *liaison*. At the <u>end</u> of a phrase it is pronounced **without** a [k] sound. However, even the venerable Fouché, in his book on French pronunciation, admits that this rule is not always followed, and that many French people pronounce the [k] at all times.

16. The [ɛ̃] nasal vowel in French <u>de-nazalizes</u> in *liaison,* except in the words *rien* and *bien.*

ACT II

1. A sistrum was an ancient Egyptian percussion instrument consisting of a lyre-shaped frame with loosely held rods running through it. It was a rattle or noisemaker that the ancient Egyptian priests of Isis used to shake at their festivals of that goddess. (From the Greek *seistron,* "to shake.")

2. *Zébré* comes from "zebra," an animal with stripes as well.

3. *Faire rage* is an expression meaning "to use maximum strength," "to do something with such energy as to seem possessed."

4. A *corregidor* in Spain was the chief magistrate of a town, the one who "corrected" bad situations, such as shutting down Pastia's tavern due to the smuggling business that went on inside.

5. *Vivat,* according to all the dictionaries, is pronounced **without** a *t* at the end. In *Werther* the two pals Johann and Schmidt praise Bacchus **IN LATIN**: *Vivat Bacchus semper vivat.* In this case the word <u>is</u> pronounced with a *t,* but not here.

6. The word *Toréador* is a French fabrication. A bullfighter in Spanish is a *torero.* The mainliner is usually called *matador* ("killer") or *espada* ("sword"). In the fourth act, Escamillo is called *espada* by the chorus.

7. It is imperative for the singer doing this role to know what a bullfight is and what goes on. The first part is the *desfile,* the procession, where the leading Matador (Escamillo) enters

the arena, followed by his *quadrilla* (his "team"); this "team" consists of helpers, all bullfighters but not as famous or brave as the leading Matador. The *banderilleros*, men with the barbed darts (*banderillas*; in French, *banderilles*) colorfully decorated, are also part of the team. When the trumpet sounds, the bull-pen (**toril**) is opened, and the raging bull (who has been in darkness for two days) bounds out into the light, accosting anything or anyone it sees in its path. Its fury is unbounded. The lesser bullfighters, using a large cape, test the bull's reactions, trying to see which way he hooks his horns, while the Matador watches. He may himself then make a few passes with the *capa*, the cape, to see how the bull behaves. At this point comes what is considered the cowardly portion of the bullfights, when the **picadors** enter the arena, on blindfolded, well-padded horses, and by deft maneuvers attract the bull to their mounts; *picadors* are usually older bullfighters, who have lost either their nerve or their agility and reflexes. As the bull charges, they prick the big neck muscle on its back with a long pointed lance called a *pica* (ergo: <u>pica</u>dors). After several jabs with the lance, the bull's neck muscles are sufficiently weakened so that his whole head is now lower. Once the bullfight "president" deems that enough damage has been caused by the *picadors*, he orders them off. Now come the **banderilleros**, who with deft footwork attract the bull to them, and just as it charges, they elegantly avoid the rush and stick the barbed *banderillas* into the same neck muscle. Three, sometimes four, pairs of *banderillas* (depending on the bull's bravery or the Matador's request) are stuck into the bleeding animal, now totally confused, enraged, and weakened by the loss of blood. Now comes the part of the spectacle where the Matador shows his skill and bravery. He uses a short red cape called a *muleta*, and exposing himself with uncommon fearlessness, he performs his cape work (called *faena*) until the panting bull is so exhausted that it just stands there, head lowered. This is "the moment of truth." The Matador takes his sword, which up to now was wrapped in his cape, and he places himself motionless before the bull. He aims his sword and lunges forward with great bravery between the bull's horns and plunges his sword into the back of the neck of the bull, hopefully avoiding a sudden upward surge of the bull's head, which could be fatal for him. If the thrust is true, the bull should fall dead on the spot. Sometimes the operation has to be repeated, depending on the bullfighter's skill (or courage). The bull's body is then dragged off the arena by teams of mules. If the president and the public deem the fight to have been extraordinary, the bullfighter is awarded the tail and ears. Much noise attends these affairs, and dark-eyed *señoritas* are seen everywhere, wearing their *mantillas*, glancing admiringly at the handsome, brave *matador.*

8. The *Toril* is the bull-pen, where the fierce bull has been kept in darkness for some time. As the door is lifted, he sees the bright light and rushes out in all his fury.

9. The *banderillas* are short lances about three feet long, ending in a fish-hook sort of point, that once having penetrated the animal's flesh are very hard to dislodge. These *banderillas* are adorned with multi-colored ornaments along the length of the shaft.

10. The letter *d* in *liaison* always becomes a *t*.

11. At the end of the words *tromperie, duperie, volerie* the scores show a very short grace note intended for the mute *e*. Tempi vary according to conductors, but in no way should the singer try to sing **any** mute *e*.

12. The only word change in this section is **les belles**, instead of *mes belles* the time before, when the men were singing alone.

13. Alcalá de Henares is a small village in Spain and is the birthplace of Cervantes.

14. Remember there is no [k] sound when *donc* is at the end of a sentence!

15. *Se mettre en quatre*, literally, "go get oneself on all fours," by extension, "work hard," "go out of one's way."
16. The troop of dragoons to which José belongs wears **canary** yellow uniforms. In her fury Carmen is also calling him a coward, <u>yellow</u>, like the color of his uniform.
17. In the Alkor-Edition score, Carmen in a mocking way repeats José's text, albeit in a lower key.

ACT III

1. *Haut* is a word beginning with an "aspirate *h*," and therefore, according to perhaps one of the strictest rules, **no** *liaison* is allowed from the preceding word. If the *liaison* were made by mistake, it would change the meaning of the phrase to "in the water," instead of "above" (*en eau* [ã‿'no]). Pierre Bernac, in his book *The Interpretation of French Song*, states that "whenever a *liaison* <u>changes the meaning of a sentence</u>, or <u>creates confusion</u>, it is better **not** to elide." In the case above we have to follow the strict rule that *liaison* is **never** made before words beginning with an <u>aspirate *h*</u>; *haut* is such a word. Look up *h* words in a good French dictionary. If the *h* is preceded by an asterisk or other mark, it signifies <u>aspirate *h*</u>. If there is no such asterisk then you will know that it is a <u>mute *h*</u> word, and *liaison* and élision are safely allowed.
2. There is a rule concerning *liaison* that <u>nouns in the singular</u> must not be elided to the next word. Since *chemin* is a noun meaning "path," we cannot say [ʃœmẽ‿'nɛ 'librœ]. However, this rule about "nouns in the singular" has its many exceptions, as we will see, and French singers often make unbelievable mistakes in this regard. Many a time in my career have I seen French people locking horns with each other on matter of *liaison*. One respected French singer in his book on French song <u>specifically</u> forbids a certain *liaison*, and in his recording of the same piece he unbelievable **makes it**!

3. This is a special case where by saying ['krwa‿tɔnɛ‿tɔœ] we create a phonetic situation with a comical alliteration of the juxtaposed *t*'s. This is frowned upon. Therefore the *liaison* **is** allowed, but with **A SLIGHT**, ever so gentle *t*. The phrase would certainly <u>not</u> suffer if it were made <u>without</u> the *t liaison*.

4. Make sure to emphasize the two *f*'s. *Un chef fameux.*

5. Notice that there is **no** *liaison* with a **t** between *sert* and *rien*. You will hear famous French singers making that bad *liaison* sometimes. Ignore it! In situations where the word ends in ***rt***, ***rd***, ***rs***, it is THE SOUNDED consonant that it goes across and NOT the silent one.

6. No *liaison* in this case because these are two sentences independent of each other: *Prenez les ballots* ("Take the bales") *et partons* ("and let us leave").

7. We must avoid a "comical alliteration" with three successive *t*'s: [tu‿tetɛ]. For this reason we eliminate the middle *liaison*.

8. Here we have a case of "suspicious" *liaison* being avoided because the word *suis* is sung on too long a note to make the *liaison* with the *z* acceptable. Also, since Escamillo is not such a common French name, we wouldn't want someone to think (by making the *liaison* with the *z*) that his name was Zescamillo! In *Werther* we will encounter *Albert*, a much more common name, and in that instance a *liaison* will be allowed.

9. *Pouvoir y rester*, literally "to stay there," "not to be able to leave," and by extension, **dead**.

10. *Navaja* is a Spanish switchblade knife, usually kept on the belt.

11. ***Corrida de toros*** is Spanish for "bullfight." In Spanish one usually refers to the spectacle as *una corrida*.

12. The pronouns *quelqu'un* and *chacun* <u>do not</u> elide the final *n* to make a *liaison*.

ACT IV

1. Old copper Spanish coin, valued at **one quarter** of the main currency.

2. The *quadrille* in bullfighting is the "team" that follows the bullfighter, consisting of his *picadors*, *banderilleros*, *chulos* ("helpers"), and other necessary personnel. They parade into the arena amid great fanfare and applause.

3. It is a common sight in eagerly awaited *corridas* to see the spectators toss their hats and caps in the air in a gesture of excitement.

4. *Alguazil* (in Spanish, *alguacil*) is a minor law enforcement officer. In this case it refers to the policeman.

5. The *chulos* are the bullfighter's helpers, who usually use their large capes to test the bull's first reactions after he bounds out of the *toril*. At this point it is a good time to explain the French pronunciation of some of these Spanish terms. First of all, the word *toréador* is a French, not Spanish, term, as explained in note 6, Act II. The Spanish word is *torero*. In Escamillo's "toreador song," he says *oui les toréros*. The final *s* is not pronounced because the word has become a part of the French language and is accepted pronounced without the final *s*, as it is in Spanish. However, in the other Spanish terms encountered in this opera, the final *s* is pronounced: **quartos̲**, **señoras̲, caballeros̲, sombreros̲, chulos̲, banderilleros̲**.

6. The men with their *banderillas*, short barbed lances gaily decorated with ribbons, intended to be harpooned into the bull's neck muscle.

7. A bullfighter's outfit is called *traje de luces* (literally, "a suit of lights"). It is fit close to the body and is lavishly embroidered in colorful patterns that catch the light of the afternoon sun, the time for *corridas*.

8. These are the men entrusted with humbling the bull's bravery by digging their *picas* or lances from atop a well-padded, blindfolded horse. They are usually older men, probably

former *toreros* who have simply become too old to perform as headliners.

9. I have never seen a "handsome" picador. They are usually rather heavy-set and paunchy!

10. By now, after my repeated notes on the art of bullfighting, it is **not** the flanks of the bull the *picadors* aim at, but the big neck muscle right behind his head. They do this in order to weaken the muscle and force the bull to keep his head down.

11. This is the name also given the headline *matador*. Literally it means "the sword," referring to the curved sword with which only he will kill the bull at "the moment of truth."

12. *Harceler* is a word beginning with an "aspirate *h*," and therefore **no** *liaison* is permitted! Every French dictionary worth its salt will show an aspirate *h* word with an (*) asterisk before it. If there is no asterisk, then *liaison* is allowed.

    homme   *harceler
    heure   *harpe
    haleine   *haine

13. The rule says specifically that the [k] sound in *donc* at the end of a sentence, even though followed by an exclamation sign, is **not pronounced**! Undoubtedly one hears Carmens (even French Carmens) saying the final [k]. See note 15, Act I. It remains a moot point of French diction, as this phrase is spat out with much vehemence, and maybe a [k] at the end is dramatically more effective.